The

Knocking

at the

Door

By: Robert J. Wieland

First Edition, 1983 © Robert J. Wieland
Copyright CFI Book Division 2023

Published by CFI Book Division
P.O. Box 159, Gordonsville, Tennessee 38563

ISBN: 979-8-9892954-0-1

Table of Contents

Key To Abbreviations Used

Key	Book Title
AA	*Acts of the Apostles*
BC	*The Seventh-day Adventist Bible Commentary*, Vols. 1-7
COL	*Christ's Object Lessons*
CT	*Counsels to Parents, Teachers and Students*
CWE	*Counsels to Writers and Editors*
DA	*The Desire of Ages*
Ev	*Evangelism*
EW	*Early Writings*
FCE	*Fundamentals of Christian Education*
GC	*The Great Controversy*
GW	*Gospel Workers*
MOD	*Movement of Destiny*
ML	*My Life Today*
PK	*Prophets and Kings*
PP	*Patriarchs and Prophets*
QOD	*Seventh-day Adventists Answer Questions on Doctrine*
R&H	*The Advent Review and Sabbath Herald*
SC	*Steps to Christ*
SM	*Selected Messages*
ST	*The Signs of the Times*
T	*Testimonies for the Church*, Vols. 1-9
TM	*Testimonies to Ministers and Gospel Workers*
YI	*The Youth's Instructor*

INTRODUCTION

If Jesus Himself were guest speaker in your church this coming Sabbath, what would His message be?

The answer is simple. He is Guest Speaker already; and His message is readily available for all to hear — the message addressed "unto the angel of the church of the Laodiceans."

Probably more sermons have been preached among us and more words written about the Laodicean message than any other single topic for the past hundred years. Yet for some strange reason, the change the message calls for seems never to have taken place. As the decades roll on relentlessly, it appears that the tragic spiritual conditions that call for change have become even more serious.

Has the familiar language of Revelation 3:14-21 become so common to us that it is blase? Do we flog ourselves with periodic harangues based on this message until we have become bored with the masochistic ritual?

When will the last sermon on the Laodicean message be preached that will result in *action* that fulfills the "counsel" given by the True Witness?

This book is not intended to be a rehash of tired cliches applied in a fault-finding spirit. We will look at our Lord's message from an uncommon perspective — that of the 1888 message of Christ's righteousness. The familiar words of Jesus to the seventh church may take on a new and startling significance in the light of our post-1888 history. They become "present truth."

It is God's plan that truth shall bring His people into a perfect working unity. May the principles presented here help us all to unite upon the foundation of eternal truth, so that we can learn to glorify our Lord both as individuals and as a body, and truly *act* upon His "counsel" in the Laodicean message. Strident voices tell us there is no hope for the church; there is hope if we will *do* what our Lord says: "Be zealous therefore, and repent."

———————

History is no sad paean of woe; it is rather a reiterated call to repentance.
— G. Ernest Wright, *The Challenge of Israel's Faith*

The Lord has declared that the history of the past shall be rehearsed as we enter upon the closing work.
— Ellen G. White, MS 129, 1905 (2SM 390)

We cannot escape history. In the long run there is no appeal from history to any higher court for the simple reason that history has been woven on God's loom.
— Abraham Lincoln

Again and again I have been shown that the past experiences of God's people are not to be counted as dead facts. We are not to treat the record of these experiences as we would treat a last year's almanac. The record is to be kept in mind; for history will repeat itself.
— Ellen G. White, MS. D-238, 1903

1

Our Seventh-day Adventist
Impasse

There is a neglected but essential preparation to make before the final outpouring of the Holy Spirit in the Latter Rain can possibly come. The solution to our problem may be far more simple than we have supposed. That most necessary preparation is a clear understanding of Christ's special message to His people in the last days — the Laodicean message addressed to the "angel" of the seventh church of Revelation 2 and 3.

Although it is true that "the Laodicean message ... must go to all the churches" (6T 77), Ellen G. White applies it primarily and especially to the Seventh-day Adventist denomination over and over again. Further, when the Seventh-day Adventist Church understands and receives that message, she says, "the loud cry of the third angel" will no longer be delayed. We acknowledge that the Latter Rain and Loud Cry *have* been delayed for many decades. The only possible conclusion is that there must be something in the Laodicean message which we have not understood or received. Consider this significant statement:

> I was shown that the testimony to the Laodiceans applies to God's people at the present time, and the reason it has not accomplished a greater work is because of the hardness of their hearts. ... When it was first presented, ... nearly all believed [correctly, it is implied] that this message would end in the loud cry of the third angel. ... It is designed to arouse the people of God, to discover to them their backslidings,

and to lead to zealous repentance, that they may be favored with the presence of Jesus, and be fitted for the loud cry of the third angel. (1T 186).

If, after all these many decades of praying for it, we are still not "fitted for the loud cry," would it not be wisdom to turn our attention to the Laodicean message in order to find the reason? Perhaps we have not grasped "this message in all its phases" (7BC 964). Is it wise for us to assume that we already understand the deep import of that message? The following points to an experience still future:

> The message to the Laodicean church is highly applicable to us as a people. It has been placed before us for a long time, but has not been heeded as it should have been. When the work of repentance is earnest and *deep*, the individual members of the church will buy the rich goods of heaven. (7BC 961; 1894; emphasis added).

> ... There is a dead fly in the ointment. ... Your self-righteousness is nauseating to the Lord Jesus Christ. (Rev. 3:15-18 quoted.) These words apply to the churches and to many of those in positions of trust in the work of God. (*Ibid.*, 962, 963; 1899).

There is a profound and mysterious link that relates the 1888 message to Christ's appeal to His beloved Laodicea. We see that times almost without number Ellen G. White tied these two together. For example, consider the following taken from a letter written in the context of the 1888 message and the reaction against it (righteousness by faith is the subject):

> The Laodicean message has been sounding. Take this message in all its phases and sound it forth to the people wherever Providence opens the way. Justification by faith and the righteousness of Christ are the themes to be presented to a perishing world. (7BC 964, 1892).

The divinely appointed remedies for the Laodicean condition of pride are "gold tried in the fire," "white raiment" and "eyesalve." These are the essential themes that made up the 1888 message. With the passage of time it becomes increasingly apparent that the remnant church has never clearly understood the dynamics of this message. Dare we deny that this pointed rebuke penned in 1890 is applicable today?

> How can our ministers become the representatives of Christ when they feel self-sufficient, when by spirit and attitude they say, "I am rich, and increased with goods, and have need of nothing"? We must not be in a self-satisfied condition, or we shall be described as those who are poor, and wretched, and miserable, and blind, and naked.

> Since the time of the Minneapolis meeting, I have seen the state of the Laodicean Church as never before. I have heard the rebuke of God spoken to those who feel so well satisfied, who know not their spiritual destitution ... like the Jews, many have closed their eyes lest they should see, but there is as great peril now in closing the eyes to light and in walking apart from Christ, feeling need of nothing, as there was when He was upon earth ...

> Those who realize their need of repentance toward God, and faith toward our Lord Jesus Christ will have contrition of soul, will repent for their resistance of the Spirit of the Lord. They will confess their sin in refusing the light that Heaven has so graciously sent them, and they will forsake the sin that grieved and insulted the Spirit of the Lord. (R&H, August 26, 1890).

If the Laodicean message is designed that the church "be fitted for the loud cry of the third angel" (1T 186), and "the state of the Laodicean church" "since the time of the Minneapolis meeting" is said to be perilous "as never before" (*op. cit.*), it is obvious that here is a field of study deserving our closest attention. In the simple fact that the Loud Cry has not yet gone forth as it should, history demonstrates that here is "present truth." Our present concern for finding the real cause for the long delay must lead us to a restudy of the message of Christ to the Laodicean church.

If we feel "rich and increased with goods" in regard to our understanding of "righteousness by faith," and if we feel proud and satisfied because of our great progress in proclaiming it to the world, we shall feel no heart-need to study the Laodicean message. But the True Witness assures us that this is precisely our greatest danger. The failure to *realize* — this is our problem.

But if we sense a tremendous "hunger and thirst after righteousness," if we have a deep conviction that history has brought us to a place of great crisis spiritually and that the Laodicean message provides the key to unlock our present impasse, then the Laodicean message will surely be reconsidered with open-minded candor. Perhaps then in answer to fervent prayer, the Holy Spirit may be able to impress both reader and writer and bring them into a common experience of discovery and enlightenment. Surely this is God's will for us all.

The expression "gold tried in the fire" we have commonly understood to refer to the refining process of personal trials experienced — individually. This understanding has hidden the more direct application of this "counsel" corporately to the church leadership, "the angel" of the church.

Is it possible that the "fire" is a reference to the "shaking," that traumatic and cataclysmic event that will try our souls as no other experience in our history? The True Witness has listed the "gold" as the first remedy. Is it because the realization of our doctrinal and spiritual poverty is the most difficult barrier in our consciousness?

If this restudy of the Laodicean message has any validity at all, we shall all find it challenging to relate to these conclusions. Could it be that our Lord is kindly yet firmly reminding us that experiencing the unprecedented opportunities of the Latter Rain and the Loud Cry will involve trials and sacrifices as severe as fire purging gold?

2

To Whom Is The Message Addressed?

As we look at Rev. 3:14-21, several very important factors come to light:

First, we find that the message is not addressed to the laity of the church, but to its leadership. This is entirely different from the usual application made for many decades. Whereas we ministers have often pleaded with our congregations to accept this message, all the while the Lord has intended that *we* accept it. He addresses the message thus: "Unto the *angel* of the church of the Laodiceans, write …" (Rev. 3:14). How do we know that "the angel of the church" is the leadership of the church? He Himself answers:

> The mystery of the seven stars which thou sawest in My right hand, and the seven golden candlesticks. The seven stars are the angels of the seven churches, and the seven candlesticks which thou sawest are the seven churches. (Rev. 1:20).

Who are the "seven stars" that He "holdeth … in His right hand" (Rev. 2:1)? They are the ministerial leadership of the church:

> God's ministers are symbolized by the seven stars, which he who is the first and the last has under His special care and protection. The sweet influences that are to be abundant in the church are bound up with these ministers of God, who are to represent the love of Christ. The stars of heaven are under God's control. He fills them with light. He guides and directs their movements. If He did not they would become fallen stars. So with his ministers. (GW 13, 14).

The "crown of twelve stars" on the head of the pure woman represents the twelve apostles (Rev. 12:1). When the "little horn" "cast down some of the stars to the ground," we commonly understand them to symbolize prominent Jewish leaders (Dan. 8:10). The star "called Wormwood" we understand to be Attila, leader of the Huns; and "the third part of the stars" smitten by his depredations we take to be the leaders of the Roman Empire (Rev. 8:11, 12).

Church leadership is said to be especially "those in the offices that God has appointed for the leadership of His people" (AA 163, 164). It follows that the "angel of the church of the Laodiceans" is the human leadership of the church, "the great heart of the work," "the highest authority that God has upon the earth" (3T 492). It is to this leadership, therefore, that the Lord Jesus primarily addresses His all-important Laodicean message. If they truly understand and receive the message, the ministry and laity of the church will be quick to accept it also. This is implied from the following:

> The members of our churches are not incorrigible; the fault is not so much to be charged upon them as upon their teachers. Their ministers do not feed them. ("To Brethren in Responsible Positions." *Special Testimonies*, No. 10, p. 46; 1890).

Second the Lord Jesus recognizes that what has held us back is unknown sin. This is evident from several factors found in the message:

(a) He says, "I know thy works." The "angel of the church" does not know or understand his "works" or his true condition; hence the message informing him.

(b) When He says, "Thou sayest, I am rich and increased with goods, and have need of nothing," it is obvious that the "angel" does not know or realize that he says those things. In

15

fact, in the century that has passed since this message was first recognized among us as "present truth," never has a responsible Seventh-day Adventist been heard to boast in those words. Jesus must be speaking of the unconscious language of the heart. There is something more meaningful here than a superficial glance makes apparent.

(c) "Thou ... knowest not" your true condition. The Greek verb does not mean, "you know not because you have not been informed or because you have not learned," but "you know not because you have not perceived." (The negative with *oida* means a lack of perception, a lack of relationship, the equivalent of our word "unconscious").

"Thou knowest not" means that the most elementary and fundamental truths of our condition are unconscious to us. This is a lack of perception, not a lapse of conscious memory. It is not a lack of awareness due to weakened physical organisms, a lowering of the spiritual "I.Q." due to illness or degeneracy, or even a lack of mental information. It is not a lack of intelligence. *We "know not" because a spiritual and emotional barrier has been erected in our souls due to our guilt in consequence of sin.*

To recognize that the message is addressed primarily to the leadership of the church is in no way being critical. For one thing, the observation is based on simple fact. Further, it is a truth that greatly enhances the respect that is due to church leadership. Respect for the principles of church organization is inherent in this understanding of the Laodicean message. Church leadership, especially that of the General Conference, is tremendously important. To understand that "the angel of the church" is primarily General Conference leadership restores respect for church organization to its rightful place. To deny it is to invite chaos.

And, last, this recognition can in no way be considered fault-finding. This is because the principle of corporate guilt presented in this book precludes the possibility of any "holier-than-thou" attitude. We are all in this problem together, and the long delay is our total responsibility together.

3

How The "Thou Knowest Not" Problem Began

Deep guilt was created in the human soul in the Garden of Eden when our first parents fell. It is as true of us today as it was for Adam, for "in Adam all die" (1 Corinthians 15:22). All of us have repeated Adam's fall (cf. Romans 5:12).

The first result of this guilt was *shame:* "Adam and his wife hid themselves from the presence of the Lord God amongst the trees of the garden" (Genesis 3:8).

The second evidence was *fear:* "And ... Adam ... said, I heard Thy voice in the garden, and I was afraid, because I was naked; and I hid myself' (verses 9,10).

The third consequence was the erection of a *barrier* creating an unconscious condition. Adam found himself unable to realize his guilt and confess it. Thus he repressed it immediately. He blamed it all on Eve: "And the man said, The woman whom Thou gavest to be with me, she gave me of the tree and I did eat" (verse 12). The guilty pair would have died then and there had they been conscious of the full extent of their guilt, for "the wages of sin is death" (Romans 6:23). When the lost at last fully grasp the enormity of their guilt, they will suffer the second death in fulfillment of the Lord's warning to Adam and Eve that when they should sin, "thou shalt surely die" (Genesis 2:17). We need to recognize that the guilt of sin brings its own built-in penalty of eternal death, and the very fact that our physical life is extended through probationary time is prima facie evidence of the existence of an unconscious mechanism of repression which had its origin in Eden.

.

This "thou knowest not" condition was therefore a blessing, for it made continued life possible. God's purpose of course was to give man an opportunity to learn repentance and faith in a Saviour.

The fourth consequence was the development of an *enmity* against God: "The woman which *Thou* gavest to be with me ..." Adam felt that the trouble was really God's fault! Eve shared this newly erected unconscious barrier in that she also could not accept and confess her own guilt any more easily: "The *serpent* beguiled me, and I did eat" (Genesis 3:13).

Ever since that first sin in the Garden, mankind have been repeating the tragic pattern. Unless man has faith in a divine Saviour who bears the full burden of his guilt, a full realization of guilt kills him. Seen in this light, it is merciful that we do not realize our depth of sin and guilt. This condition of "thou knowest not" could go on forever and ever, except that there must come a second advent of Christ and there must come an end to sin. Hence the Laodicean message!

When Adam and Eve "hid themselves from the presence of the Lord God," they did so because they were hiding from themselves as well. Their new conviction of guilt was naturally unwelcome to their knowledge. We cannot overestimate the traumatic effect of this original sin and guilt upon their human souls. They just could not face themselves. For some mysterious reason they felt naked in front of each other and before God. They were different. "The Lord God walking in the garden in the cool of the day" had suddenly become to them an unwelcome interloper. They wished He would leave them alone. His presence awakened unpleasant convictions that they would fain forget.

Thus it has been with man ever since. "And even as they did not like to retain God in their knowledge, God gave them over to a reprobate mind" (Rom. 1:28).

The knowledge of God was repressed because it awakened the intolerable sense of guilt from which man longed to escape. Thus it was driven into deep hiding. This function of repression as consequent on guilt is alluded to by Paul: "We see divine retribution revealed from heaven and falling upon all the godless wickedness of men. In their wickedness *they are stifling the truth*. For all that may be known of God by men lies plain before their eyes; indeed God Himself has disclosed it to them … But all their thinking has ended in futility, and their misguided minds are plunged in darkness" (Rom. 1:18-21 NEB, emphasis added).

"Yes," someone may say at this point, "but all this refers to the wicked. They have these problems, not we. We are born-again Christians and we don't have any problem with repressed guilt as they do. The blood of Jesus Christ has already cleansed us from all this!" But our Lord, the "Faithful and True Witness," says that we too have a problem with unknown sin: "Thou knowest not" your true condition, He says. Something has delayed the coming of the Lord and held up the Loud Cry for decades in spite of the fact that we are such sincere, born-again Christians!

The sinful Adam in the Garden had a problem with "enmity against God." Could we, nearly six thousand years away from him, have the root of the same problem and not be aware of it? "The carnal mind is enmity against God," says Paul (Rom. 8:7). Until the people of God are truly ready for the sealing and the close of probation, they most certainly do have a problem. If we keep going into our graves as have countless generations before us ever since Eden, we are continually taking our problem with us to the grave. Not until the problem is solved can God's people possibly be prepared to "stand in the sight of a holy God without a mediator" (GC 425). Not until there is "a special work of purification, of putting away of sin among God's people upon earth," can we assume that alienation is really overcome.

Latent "enmity against God" is the root of the problem. This is what has created a need for a "final atonement." But we just don't see it. It is an unconscious sin. We are like our beloved brother Peter. Years after his baptism and his ordination to the ministry and after years of schooling under Christ Himself, Peter did not know or understand his own hidden motivations:

> When Peter said he would follow his Lord to prison and to death, he meant it, every word of it but he did not know himself. Hidden in his heart were elements of evil that circumstances would fan into life. Unless he was made conscious of his danger, these would prove his eternal ruin. The Saviour saw in him a self-love and assurance that would overbear his Love for Christ. ... Christ's solemn warning was a call to heart searching. (DA 673).

Could words more plainly say that Peter's problem lay in his unknown heart? As our Saviour beholds us now, on the eve of our last great trial, what does He see hidden in our hearts that must be "made conscious" to us?

When Peter finally denied his Lord, he did that which none of us dare repeat in the final test when "the righteous must live in the sight of a holy God without an intercessor?:

> Peter had just declared that he knew not Jesus, but he now realized with bitter grief how well his Lord knew him, and how accurately He had read his heart, the falseness of which was unknown even to himself. (DA 713).

And yet Peter was a truly sincere "born-again Christian." Thank God the final tests have not come as yet! Who of us would truly be ready?

The original sin of Adam and Eve was to the cross at Calvary what the acorn is to the oak. The seed or resentment against

God is evident in Adam's statement blaming Him. But Adam would have been horrified had he fully realized how this seed would grow into the eventual murder of the Son of God. He would have been unable to endure the full disclosure of the real dimensions of his guilt. The sacrificial victim offered in the Garden outlined for Adam the dimmest shadow of the cross, for he "saw Christ prefigured in the innocent beast suffering the penalty of his transgression of Jehovah's law" (6BC 1095). And "he trembled at the thought that his sin must shed the blood of the spotless lamb of God. This scene gave him a deeper and more vivid sense of the greatness of his transgression, which nothing but the death of God's dear Son could expiate" (PP 68). But the full consciousness of their sin and guilt was veiled from the guilty couple:

> After Adam and Eve had partaken of the forbidden fruit, they were filled with a sense of shame and terror. At first their only thought was, how to excuse their sin before God, and escape the dreaded sentence of death. ...The spirit of self-justification originated in the father of lies, and has been exhibited by all the sons and daughters of Adam. (5T 637, 638).

It is fortunate that ever since the Fall man's guilt has remained partly unconscious because if it were fully conscious it would kill him. Hence the Creator's kindly sentence, "In the day that thou eatest thereof *dying thou shalt die*" (Gen. 2:17, mg.). Had Adam and Eve been fully conscious of their guilt in the Garden, it would have killed them outright as it killed Christ on His cross. Not until He came did anyone fully sense it. Only "He was made to be sin for us who knew no sin" (2 Cor. 5:21).

The real reason why we do things is often veiled from us. Because recognition of the true motive would horrify us, we "stifle the truth" as Paul says. We can believe ever so sincerely that we act out of a sense of justice when in reality we may be motivated by cruelty. We can sincerely believe that we are motivated by love and yet be driven instead by a self-centered craving for acceptance. We can believe that duty is our guide when our main motivation is vanity. We can believe that we stand secure in "righteousness by faith" when in reality an egocentric concern is driving us to seek personal security and we are in fact "under the law," ignorant of genuine New Testament faith. We can fondly imagine that we are truly constrained by the love of Christ when we don't really comprehend "what is the breadth, and length, and depth, and height" of that love and are therefore most certainly living unto ourselves, the very thing the cross was intended to make impossible "henceforth" (cf. 2 Cor. 5:14, 15).

These rationalizations can be very self-deceiving. And the more ardently we want to protect ourselves from coming face to face with our true motivations, the more desperately we must make ourselves believe in our mistaken assumptions. And yet the existence of this "thou knowest not" state is not something so hidden from us that we cannot recognize the problem is there. It can readily be glimpsed if we will look at ourselves candidly, and accept the Word of God sincerely and intelligently.

The ultimate self-deception, of course, is reached when God's people, and especially their spiritual leadership, believe they are motivated by a wholesome desire to preserve "the nation," but crucify the Christ from the real motivation of "enmity against God." Thus "they know not what they do" (Luke 23:34). And the sad day also comes centuries later when the leaders of God's people sincerely believe they are motivated by a desire to "stand by the old landmarks" and preserve the old-time "third angel's message" when in reality they reject the beginning of the Latter Rain and the Loud Cry. Thus, again, in 1888, "they know not what they do."

Again, decades later, another form of self-deception threatens us. We interpret mass baptisms in Third World countries as evidence that we have accepted the once rejected Latter Rain, and that our spiritual condition is therefore satisfactory. Thus, once again we virtually boast of being "rich and increased with goods [church growth], ... [in] need of nothing." According to the Laodicean message, then, the Saviour is still praying for us, "Father, forgive them, for they know not what they do."

We have seen that it was at the Fall that this barrier of unconscious guilt began. Was there such a thing in Christ when He became man? Sent "in the likeness of sinful flesh," did he inherit this barrier that hides from us the reality of our true guilt?

No. For Him there was no such barrier. "He knew all men and needed not that any should testify of man: for He knew what was in man" (John 2:24, 25). No one else has ever known, not the full depths. All through His ministry this painful knowledge burdened Him:

> And Jesus knowing their thoughts said, Wherefore think ye evil in your hearts?" (Matt. 9:4).

> "Jesus knew their thoughts ... (Matt. 12:25) "He knew their thoughts ..." (Luke 6:8).

On several occasions we find Him telling His most faithful and trusted disciples that they did not know their own hearts. "Ye know not what ye ask" (Matt. 20:22). When James and John wished to call down fire from heaven as retribution on the hapless Samaritans who had in prejudice turned Jesus away, they sincerely thought they were motivated by a righteous zeal. In a declaration parallel to the one He makes to the angel of the church of the Laodiceans, Jesus said: "Ye know not what manner of spirit ye are of" (Luke 9:55). Like ourselves, these godly apostles, unquestionably the best men in the world, were victims of their own unknowing. Using Ellen G. White's frequent and apt phase, they had "changed leaders" and did not know it.

Truly, the human "heart is deceitful above all things, and desperately wicked: who can know it?" (Jer. 17:9). Only Christ could fully know it; and what He knew finally killed Him on Calvary's cross. No merciful barrier blacked out His consciousness of our sin. He was made "to be sin for us, who knew no sin ..." (2 Cor. 5:21).

4

Unconscious Guilt
In Scripture History

The existence of unconscious repressed guilt is taught all through the Bible.

1. As a clear example of self-deceived unconscious motivations mentioned above, look again at the crucifixion of Christ Himself. The Jewish leaders were pathetically sincere in believing that the very existence of the "whole nation" required that Jesus die. Caiaphas said: "It is expedient for us, that one man should die for the people, and that the whole nation perish not. And this spake he not of himself ..." (John 11:50, 51).

These men knew full well they were crucifying an innocent man. What they "knew not" was that they were giving expression to the unconscious "enmity against God" buried beneath the surface in all carnal human hearts. Their words and actions were being motivated by an unknown force within them. We all have the same problem:

> That prayer of Christ for His enemies embraced *the world*. It took in *every sinner* that had lived or should live, from the beginning of the world to the end of time. Upon *all* rests the guilt of crucifying the Son of God. (DA 745, emphasis added).

Paul agrees that the sin of crucifying Christ was an unconscious one: "Had they known it, they would not have crucified the Lord of glory" (1 Cor. 2:8).

As in the case of the Jewish leaders, humanity today is not conscious of that guilt. But their sin is also our sin, for the simple reason that we all partake of a common humanity. We are all "members of the body".

> Let us all remember that we are still in a world where Jesus, the Son of God, was rejected and crucified, where the guilt of despising Christ and preferring a robber rather than the spotless Lamb of God still rests. ... The whole world stands charged today with the deliberate rejection and murder of the Son of God. ... All classes and sects who reveal the same spirit of envy, hatred, prejudice, and unbelief manifested by those who put to death the Son of God would act the same part, were the opportunity granted, as did the Jews and people of the time of Christ. They would be partakers of the same spirit that demanded the death of the Son of God. (TM 38).

If we refuse this clear-cut truth, we may well set the clock back for another generation. Spiritual pride evades this revelation. "Impossible! I could never do that," one may insist. Yet this was precisely the proud assumption of those who rejected the beginning of the Loud Cry (see R&H, April 11, 1893).

The final unfolding of history will be the disclosure of the world's guilt so that all can see it at last. When the world unites to exterminate the people of God in the final decree, this unconscious mind of evil will be fully manifest. No longer will the Holy Spirit restrain it. And their hatred of God's people will be in reality hatred of Christ — a fresh and complete display of the same unconscious hatred manifested at Calvary, "that all the world may become guilty [out in the open] before God" (Rom. 3:19).

The painful truth disclosed in the True Witness's message to the "angel of the church of the Laodiceans" is that a related guilt is our real sin today. And it is holding up the Latter Rain. Beneath the surface there is a "carnal mind" which "is enmity against God." All through the decades this unconscious enmity against God has frustrated our best conscious efforts to hasten the coming of the Lord.

Obviously, only the "blotting out of sins" accomplished in the Day of Atonement can avail to cleanse this deeper level of unknown sin. When this work is done, the mysterious phrase, "the final atonement," will be better appreciated. No magical process will do the work The now unknown sins will be brought fully to consciousness and forthwith repented of. But this will not be possible unless side by side with the abounding awareness of our sin there is a "more abounding" awareness of what grace really means. Hence the necessity for a clearer understanding of the gospel than we have ever known before — righteousness by faith. The "enmity" fully healed, the "atonement" becomes fully effective or "final." It is, in fact, a final reconciliation.

2. Long before Calvary Jesus pointed out the unconscious sin of His enemies:

> Therefore speak I to them in parables: because they seeing see not; and hearing they hear not, neither do they understand. And in them is fulfilled the prophecy of Esaias, which saith, By hearing ye shall hear, and shall not understand; and seeing ye shall see, and shall not perceive [*oida*, be conscious:] For this people's heart is waxed gross, and their ears are dull of hearing and their eyes they have closed; lest at any time they should see with their eyes, and hear with their ears, and should understand with their heart, and should be converted, and I should heal them. (Matt. 13: 13-15).

Mark adds in place of the last phrase, "lest at any time they should be converted, and their sins should be forgiven them" (Mark 4:12). Thus the thing not "known" (*oida*) is shown to be their sins. The divine Agency whose work it is to bring unrealized sin to consciousness is the Holy Spirit: "And when He is come, He will reprove [convict] the world of sin" (John 16:8). It is impossible for such sin to be forgiven until the Holy

Spirit imparts a consciousness of it. This is why there can be no automatic scrubbing of the tape by pressing the magic button — "Lord, forgive me of all my sins" — without those sins coming to consciousness.

A. T. Jones, one of the agents used by the Lord to communicate to His people the "beginning" of the Latter Rain in 1888, emphasized that the sins buried in the human heart must come to our consciousness before they can be blotted out. The "good news" is that the Lord will do the work if we let Him:

> Now some of the brethren here have done that very thing. They came here free; but the Spirit of God brought up something they never saw before. The Spirit of God went deeper than it ever went before, and revealed things they never saw before; and then, instead of thanking the Lord that that was so, and letting the whole wicked business go … they began to get discouraged...

> If the Lord has brought up sins to us that we never thought of before, that only shows that He is going down to the depths, and He will reach the bottom at last; and when He finds the last thing that is unclean or impure, that is out of harmony with His will, and brings that up, and shows that to us, and we say, "I would rather have the Lord than that" — then the work is complete, and the seal of the living God can be fixed upon that character. [Congregation: "Amen".]

> This is the blessed work of sanctification. And we know that that work of sanctification is going on in us. If the Lord should take away our sins without our knowing it what good would it do us? That would be simply making machines of us. He does not propose to do that; consequently, He wants you and me to know when our sins go, that we may know when His righteousness comes. It is when we yield ourselves that we have Him. (*General Conference Bulletin*, 1893, p. 404).

In this connection we may look at the following from Ellen G. White:

> God's law reaches the feelings and motives, as well as the outward acts. It reveals the secrets of the heart flashing light upon things buried in darkness. God knows every thought, every purpose, every plan, every motive. The books of heaven record the sins that would have been committed had there been opportunity ... God has a perfect photograph of every man's character and this photograph He compares with His law. He reveals to man the defects that mar this life, and calls upon him to repent and turn from sin. (5 BC 1085).

"The things buried in darkness" are clearly not "known sins" consciously concealed from others. They are said to be "sins that would have been committed had there been opportunity." Therefore they are not sins that have been committed. These are "purposes" and "motives" buried deep within the heart. How can the final blotting out of sins possibly take place if these things never come to consciousness? It is with these things that the Laodicean message is concerned, and this is why it will "end in the loud cry of the third angel" once it is understood and gladly received as the Lord intends.

3. Thus two important factors condition the "blotting out of sins": the sins coming fully to consciousness; and a new appreciation of the cross that provides the dynamic that makes the experience possible. Take away the atonement provided at the cross and no sin whatever can be forgiven, much less "blotted out," Zechariah's great prophecy is clearly concerned with the "blotting out of sins," for he speaks of cleansing from "sin and uncleanness." This prophecy has never yet been fulfilled:

> And I will pour upon the house of David [the church leadership] and upon the inhabitants of Jerusalem [the church], the spirit of grace and of supplications; and they shall look upon Me whom they have pierced, and they shall

mourn for Him, as one mourneth for his only son, and shall be in bitterness for Him, as one that is in bitterness for his firstborn. ... In that day there shall be a fountain opened to the house of David and to the inhabitants of Jerusalem for sin and for uncleanness. (Zech. 12: 10; 13:1).

This prophecy will be partially fulfilled in the experience of those specially resurrected who actually murdered Christ at His first advent (DA 580). However, the "cleansing" brought to view as contingent on this contrite vision of Christ crucified cannot apply to them. Therefore we can expect the Holy Spirit to be "poured" upon the church leadership and upon the church, giving a new vision of Christ crucified, revealing our own participation in the crime.

"The spirit of grace and of supplications" can be none other than the Holy Spirit who "maketh intercession for the saints according to the will of God" (Rom. 8:26). In His office work of glorifying Christ (John 16:14), the Spirit will arouse in the hearts of God's people a new sense of oneness with Christ. It will be a sympathy with Him closer than one's love of an only child. This will make possible a completely new motivation for finishing the work: not a concern for our getting to Heaven, but a concern for His vindication, that He receive His reward.

Is this guilt of "piercing" Christ something that the "house of David" and the "inhabitants of Jerusalem" have been conscious of! Obviously not. The consciousness is only brought to light by the "pouring" out of the Spirit. When the Lord says "they *shall* look upon Me whom they *have* pierced," it is clear that the knowledge of this sin or of their participation in it had not previously been clearly realized.

If one will read *Testimonies to Ministers*, pages 91-96, he will see that the uplifting of Christ in the 1888 message would have fulfilled Zechariah's prophecy had the message been received by the "house of David." Certain it is that in our day this truth is not yet clearly seen by our ministry or our people. Zechariah's prophecy is yet future, and so is the ultimate "cleansing" associated with the "pouring" out of the Spirit. When it comes it will not only take care of "sin" but also "uncleanness".

Before we consider just how Laodicea's root problem is an unconscious one, how enmity against God has been and still is today the underlying barrier to receiving the outpouring of the Holy Spirit, let us turn again to our Bibles to consider more thoroughly the reality of this problem of unconscious sin.

5

When All Unrighteousness is Truly Cleansed

Some may be reticent to concur that the church has a problem as serious as this. They are impressed by 1 John 1:9, "If we confess our sins, He is faithful and just to forgive us our sins, and to cleanse us from all unrighteousness." "Lord, forgive us all our sins," they pray, assuming that each oft-repeated routine prayer "scrubs the tape." The idea that there is still something on the tape that we haven't heard yet is too shocking to believe.

If we think of the forgiveness of sins as only a preparation for death and the resurrection, we need not be concerned about unconscious sin still lurking beneath the surface. But we live in the time of the cleansing of the sanctuary. Since 1844 a new and different work has been in progress — a cleansing work, a restoration, a purification, a vindication. We are not concerned merely about getting ready to die. We are concerned about getting ready for translation. Deeper, more thorough work must be done than has been accomplished for any previous generation. The Latter Rain ripens the grain for the harvest, and "the harvest is the end of the world." Therefore, receiving the Latter Rain must lead on to a preparation for translation.

In order to understand the Laodicean message correctly, therefore, we must search in our Bibles to see that unconscious sin has been a constant problem to Gods people in past ages.

1. Many Bible statements are meaningless apart from understanding that they refer to this unknown sin. Jeremiah says, "Deep is a man's mind, deeper than all else, on evil bent;

who can fathom it?" (Jer. 17:9, Moffatt). It would seem that Paul had this statement in mind when he said, "The carnal mind is enmity against God." And this "enmity" is the depth which cannot be "fathomed". The mind conceals its true motivations from our awareness. The KJV adds, "I the Lord search the heart I try the reins" (verse 10). "Reins" is a Hebrew figure of speech that is difficult to understand apart from recognizing the unconscious motivations of the heart.*

"The righteous God trieth the hearts and *reins*" (Ps. 7:9). "Thou hast possessed my *reins*. ... *Search me*, O God, and know my heart: try me, and know my thoughts: and see if there be any wicked way in me (Ps. 139:13, 23, 24). "Examine me, O Lord, and prove me; try my reins and my heart" (Ps. 26:2).

Jeremiah appeals to the Lord to vindicate his true motives: "O Lord of hosts, that judges righteously, that triest the *reins* and the heart ... unto thee have I revealed my cause" (Jer. 11:20).

This thought of disclosing the hidden motivations of the heart is carried over into the New Testament. Because the Lord alone "searcheth the reins and hearts," He will "give unto every one of you according to your works" (Rev. 2:23). Thus when the Lord later says to Laodicea, "I know thy works," it is clear that the Laodicean message is also a "searching of the reins and

---

* The "reins" is an idiom of both Hebrew and New Testament Greek de-noting the kidneys. As the ancients were relatively unacquainted with the functions of physiology, the kidneys symbolized for them the unknown depths of one's feelings and emotions. Note the following from *The Expository Greek New Testament:*

"I know the abysses," and "discerner of hearts and searcher of the reins" were old Egyptian titles for divine beings. This intimate knowledge of man pierces below superficial appearances. The divine acquaintance with man's real secret life forms the basis of unerring and impartial judgment. (Vol. 5. pp. 361, 362).

hearts," a disclosing of the "things before buried in darkness," to borrow Ellen G. White's phrase quoted previously.

We have already considered how Christ did not have the same problem of an unconscious mind as we do. Isaiah says of Him:

> The Spirit of the Lord shall rest upon Him, the spirit of wisdom and understanding, the spirit of counsel and might, the spirit of knowledge and of the fear of the Lord; and shall make Him of quick understanding in the fear of the Lord: and He shall not judge after the sight of His eyes, neither reprove after the hearing of His ears. ... And righteousness shall be the girdle of His loins, and faithfulness the girdle of His *reins*. (Isa. 11:2-5).

Christ knew no repression of guilt at all. He stood before God by "faithfulness" and was thus "righteous." His motivations were pure and transparent.

> "This is but a foreshadowing of the kind of people that the third angel's message will gather out for they too are to have "the faith of Jesus"— not merely faith in Jesus, but the very kind of faith which He had, the faith *of* Jesus. This is the deep experience offered to the Laodicean church, faith, spiritual discernment and the righteousness of Christ when the door shall have been opened." (Donald K. Short, *A Study of the Cleansing of the Sanctuary in Relation to Current Denominational History*, Potomac University Masters Thesis, unpublished, 1958, p. 46).

2. David prays, "Who can understand his errors? cleanse Thou me from secret faults" (Ps. 19: 12). Obviously David is not talking about faults known to the sinner and kept secret from others. If that were the case, he would pray, "We understand our errors." He is talking about faults that the sinner himself has not yet understood. This is unconscious sin.

3. Moses prays, "Thou hast set our iniquities before Thee, our secret sins in the light of Thy countenance" (Ps. 90:8) What are these "secret sins"? Are they sins that we know about, things we cover up from others' gaze? Or are they unconscious sins? They cannot be known sins that we have confessed, for such sins are not "set ... before Thee ... in the light of Thy countenance." All such sins "Thou hast cast ... behind Thy back," "in the depths of the sea" (Isa 38:17; Micah 7:19). These must be unconfessed sins; and, in the context of Moses' prayer, they are unconscious sins.

Moses vividly describes the unconscious work of repression that operates in all sinners since the Fall: "We are consumed by Thine anger, and by Thy wrath we are troubled. ... All our days are passed away in Thy wrath: we spend our years as a tale that is told. The days of our years are threescore years and ten" (Ps. 90:7-10). Our years are a constant conflict with unrealized guilt. The Holy Spirit is constantly deepening our awareness of it. If we gladly welcome each new and deeper disclosure of our unconscious sin and readily confess it, the work of cleansing hastens on. But the work for the great body of the church has been resisted and delayed for many decades. "Thou knowest not" is still the message of the True Witness.

Our human problem of unconscious motivations was understood by Ellen G. White. In 1906 she wrote an article for the *Review* on the subject. She recognized that the subject is taught all through the Bible. She discerned how Saul of Tarsus in utter sincerity did not know his own heart, which he confessed was unknown to him. Notice in the gist of the article how she recognized that this is the great problem that man faces, and how only the ministry of Christ in the sanctuary provides the solution:

My brethren, day and night, and especially in the night season, this matter is presented to me. "Tekel; Thou art weighed in the balances and art found wanting." How do we stand before God at this time? We may be sincere, and yet greatly deceived. Saul of Tarsus was sincere when he was persecuting the church of Christ. "I verily thought," he declared, "that I ought to do many things contrary to the name of Jesus." He was sincere in his ignorance. ... We know that there is no one, however earnestly he may be striving to do his best who can say, "I have no sin." ... How then are we to escape the charge. "Thou art weighed in the balances, and art found wanting"? We are to look to Christ. At infinite cost He has convenanted to be our representative in the heavenly courts, our advocate before God.

... Weighed and found wanting is our inscription by nature. ... Let each one, old or young be faithful in dealing with himself, lest he shall stumble along in darkness, making grievous mistakes, and thus helping others to make mistakes. (*Review and Herald*, March 8, 1906).

The first part of the article is practically a Bible study on the subject of the unconscious mind. She quotes Hannah, the mother of Samuel: "... the Lord is a God of knowledge, and by Him actions are weighed' (1 Sam.. 2:3). Solomon understood how self-deceived we are: "All the ways of a man are clean in his own eyes; but the Lord weigheth the spirits" (Prov. 16:2). David discerned the problem: "Surely men of low degree are vanity, and men of high degree are a lie: to be laid in the balance, they are altogether lighter than vanity" (Ps. 62:9). Then Ellen G. White adds:

It is for the eternal interest of everyone to search his own heart and to improve every God-given faculty. Let all remember that there is not a motive in the heart of any man that the Lord does not clearly see. ... We need a connection with divine power, that we may have an increase of clear light and understanding of how to reason from cause to effect. We need to have the powers of the understanding cultivated by our being partakers of the divine nature, having escaped the corruption that is in the world through lust. ... There is not a design, however intricate, nor a motive, however carefully hidden, that He does not clearly understand. (*Ibid.*).

4. A striking example of hidden, buried sin is Hazael. He could not bring himself to believe that he was capable of doing the unspeakable things the prophet Elisha had discerned he was capable of: "I know the evil that thou wilt do unto the children of Israel: their strongholds wilt thou set on fire, and their young men wilt thou slay with the sword, and wilt dash their children, and rip up their women with child. And Hazael said, But what is thy servant a dog, that he should do this great thing?" (2 Kings 8:12, 13). Hazael was sincerely unconscious of what lay buried in his own heart. In the same way, we are sincerely unconscious of our true motivations, apart from the Holy Spirit's conviction. Note the following:

> Had anyone told them [the faultfinders] that notwithstanding their zeal and labor to set others right, they would at length be found in a similar position of darkness, they would have said, as did Hazael to the prophet "Is thy servant a dog, that he should do this great thing? (4T 89, 90).

> If when Achan yielded to temptation he had been asked if he wished to bring defeat and death into the camp of Israel, he would have answered. "No, no! is thy servant a dog, that he should do this great wickedness?" But ... he went farther than he had purposed in his heart. It is exactly in this way that individual members of the church are imperceptibly led on to ... bring the frown of God upon the church. (*Ibid.*, p. 492, 493).

Remember, as in the crucifixion of Christ, it is the motivation that is unrealized, not necessarily the outward act When we ponder how often the Lords servant likens the unconscious sin of our brethren who rejected the beginning of the Latter Rain at and following the 1888 Conference to the sin of those who rejected Christ, we begin to sense how dreadful are the consequences of the unknown sin that the True Witness would have us see. For how many decades have we been responsible for delaying the coming of the Loud Cry? All the while we have thought we were motivated by a desire to hasten His coming when in reality we have been delaying it!

5. Another classic example of the result of unknown sin is Hezekiah's experience (2 Kings 20 and 21). He had been a good king, so good that if he had said "Amen" to the Lords directive, "Set thine house in order; for thou shalt die, and not live," he would probably have gone down in sacred history as the finest king Gods people ever had. He was not aware of the hidden, buried roots of evil latent in his unconscious heart He prayed: "I beseech thee, O Lord, remember now how I have walked before thee in truth and with a perfect heart, and have done that which is good in Thy sight. And Hezekiah wept sore" (2 Kings 20:3). But his heart was not perfect! When fifteen years were added to his life, he became the victim of unconscious selfish motivations and undid all the good he had achieved in his former period of health. He begat and trained wicked Manasseh.

Jeremiah passes a retrospective judgment on the last era of his reign: Judah's national downfall came "because of Manasseh the son of Hezekiah king of Judah, for that which he did in Jerusalem" (Jer. 15:4). All the evil that Hezekiah did in those last fifteen years was already latent in his heart before his illness. "The books of heaven record the sins that would have been committed had there been opportunity" (5BC 1085).

Like good King Hezekiah, we appear to ourselves (and we try to appear to others) as if we serve the Lord "with a perfect heart." We have so long misunderstood 1 John 1:9 that we hesitate to think of the possibility of an unconscious reservoir of sin after we are "converted." "We have confessed our sins," we insist, "therefore the Lord has been faithful and just to cleanse us from all unrighteousness. There is no sin left from which we are not cleansed." What we have failed to understand is that the Lord cannot cleanse us from any unrighteousness that we have not as yet understandably confessed.

In Hezekiah's case, the Lord "left him, to try him, that he [Hezekiah] might know all that was in his heart" (2 Chron. 32:31). Inspiration says that it will be the same for the saints in the last days. They will be left to "stand in the sight of a holy God without a mediator." (GC 425 and 614). The parallel with Hezekiah is exact. But the saints dare not repeat Hezekiah's folly, for if they "should prove themselves unworthy, and lose their lives because of their own defects of character, then Gods holy name would be reproached." (GC 619).

The vindication of God, and in consequence the successful conclusion of the "great controversy between Christ and Satan," depends on their succeeding where Hezekiah failed. Would God dare to permit such a test to come before they were ready?

Hezekiah, sleeping in his grave, is a type of millions of "good" people who have died. They consciously and sincerely served the Lord as best they knew or understood. But, like Hezekiah, no generation ever understood fully the potential of their own hearts, the unconscious alienation from God that lay beneath the surface. None were required to endure the unprecedented test of living "in the sight of a holy God without an intercessor." This is because none had received "the final atonement" which alone can heal the problem of unrealized enmity against God. (The expression "final atonement" should not be relegated to the Adventist attic as a mistaken notion of naive pioneers. The expression appears rather frequently as a meaningful phrase in Ellen White's writings. There is also good evidence that Scripture upholds the idea as implicit in the magnificent concept of the cleansing of the sanctuary.)

Note, no *generation* of God's people have ever received "the final atonement." The fact that there have been a few individuals translated such as Enoch and Elijah can indicate that this experience may have been known by a scattered few in every generation.

6

Our Denominational History and the Laodicean Message

We return now to our Lords words "unto the angel of the church of the Laodiceans." He rightly assumes that we should have learned the lessons of history and that we are ready in our generation for the closing lesson preparatory to the end of history:

> These things saith the Amen, the faithful and true witness … I know thy works … Because thou sayest, I am rich, and increased with goods, and have need of nothing; and knowest not that thou art [the one] wretched, and miserable, and poor, and blind, and naked: (Rev. 3:14-17).

Not yet do we know our own "works" or history. Our history actually, as discerned by the heavenly universe, discloses our true plight as preeminently "wretched, miserable, poor, blind, and naked" of all the seven churches. (Note the use of the Greek article *ho*, "*the* one").

What is our true history? Unpleasant as the revelation may be, truth requires that it be faced honestly. Most earnest and persistent attempts have been made to identify the "they" of the following quotations as a small minority. Regrettably, the full context of Ellen G. White's writing on the subject identifies them as the bulk of the responsible leadership of the church — "the angel of the church of the Laodiceans":

> All the universe of heaven witnessed the *disgraceful treatment of Jesus Christ, represented by the Holy Spirit.* Had

Christ been before them, they would have treated Him in a manner similar to that in which the Jews treated Christ. (*Special Testimonies*, Series A, No. 6, p. 20. The context speaks of 1888; emphasis added).

We read such a statement with horror. Can it be true? How did this terrible thing happen? "This just can't be true — someone's mistaken somewhere." This is our usual attitude toward this and similar statements. "Someone find another inspired statement that cancels this one out," we plead. It is as difficult for us to face this fact as it was for Adam and Eve to face their true guilt in the Garden! But nonetheless, though we may hesitate to recognize the fact, "all the universe of heaven witnessed the disgraceful" scene.

What do the books of heaven say about this sin? According to 5BC 1085, they "record the sins that would have been committed had there been opportunity." What would our brethren have done "had Christ been before them" in 1888? The word is clear: "They would have treated Him in a manner similar to that in which the Jews treated Christ." Since the books of heaven "record the sins that would have been committed had there been opportunity," it is clear that they show that the brethren mentioned above did indeed treat Christ in a manner similar to that in which the Jews treated Him. In other words, in plain English, they "pierced Him," to borrow Zechariah's phrase!

We have tried ever so earnestly to believe that the pronoun "they" refers only to "some," a few, who treated Jesus Christ so disgracefully. One recent, highly respected denominational history describes them as "less than a score," "not even a *fourth* of the total number of participants." And of those "few," "*most* of those who first took issue made confessions within the decade following 1888, and largely within the first five years, and thenceforth ceased their opposition." (See *Movement of Destiny*, pp. 367, 368, emphasis original).

So Ellen White allowed herself to get all upset over the attitude and actions of a tiny minority of ministers, less than ten, to be exact. And she continued to fulminate against this tiny enclave of ministers for a decade, declaring that they had power to withhold from the church and the world the glorious blessings of the Latter Rain and the Loud Cry even though the vast majority of responsible leaders wholeheartedly and enthusiastically accepted the message!

Not one statement from Ellen White's pen exists in which she declares that the "some" among the responsible leadership who truly accepted the message were *many* or a *majority*. Without exception, her use of the word "some" in reference to those who accepted means "few." And above and beyond all debate on the issue looms the overwhelming fact that whatever reaction toward the 1888 message occurred, good or ill, the finishing of the work and the coming of the Lord were long delayed thereby.

Let us look briefly at some of the statements from Ellen G. White's pen which throw light on her reference to the "some":

In Minneapolis God gave precious gems of truth to His people in new settings. This light from heaven by some was rejected with all the stubbornness the Jews manifested in rejecting Christ. (MS 13, 1889; CWE 30).

Now I was saying what was the use of our assembling here together [at Minneapolis, 18881 and for our ministering brethren to come in if they are here only to shut out the Spirit of God from the people? ... I have been talking and pleading with you, but it does not seem to make any difference with you ... (MS 9, 1888).

It is not wise for one of these young men [Jones and Waggoner] to commit himself to a decision at this meeting where opposition rather than investigation is the order of the day. (MS 15, 1888)

If the ministers will not receive the light I want to give the people a chance; perhaps they may receive it. (MS 9,1888).

The really critical issue is, Are the words of our Lord in His Laodicean message present truth today? Or did the so-called "glorious" acceptance of the 1888 message by the responsible leadership of the church render this passé? Was the above statement a single out-of-character outburst of Ellen White, something that her calmer nature later repudiated? We look again. She talks about it times almost without number (all emphasis added):

Every time the same spirit [of opposition at Minneapolis] awakens in the soul, the deeds done on that occasion are endorsed, and the doers of them are made responsible to God ... *The same spirit that actuated the rejectors of Christ rankles in their hearts,* and had they lived in the days of Christ, they would have acted toward Him in a manner similar to that of the godless and unbelieving Jews. (*Special Testimonies to the Review and Herald Office,* pp. 16, 17).

If you reject Christ's delegated messengers, you *reject Christ.* (TM 96, 97. 1896).

Men professing godliness *have despised Christ* in the person of His messengers. Like the Jews, they reject Gods message. (FCE 472; 1897).

Christ has registered all the hard, proud, sneering speeches spoken against His servants *as against Himself.* (R&H. May 27, 1890).

Men among us can become just as were the Pharisees — wide-awake to condemn the greatest teacher that the world ever knew. (TM 294; 1896).

How do we know that this sin was an unconscious one? The brethren involved thought that they were reacting against an over-emphasized and erroneous message. They thought they were rejecting some fanatical, imperfect or even dangerous messengers. They thought they were "standing by the old landmarks," nobly defending the pillars of the three angels' messages. They were proud of their orthodoxy. Note how their true motivations were veiled from their knowledge:

> In Minneapolis God gave precious gems of truth to His people in new settings. This light from heaven by some was rejected with all the stubbornness the Jews manifested in rejecting Christ, and there was much talk about standing by the old landmarks. But there was evidence *they knew not* what the old landmarks were. There was evidence and there was reasoning from the word that commended itself to the conscience; but *the minds of men were fixed, sealed* against the entrance of light, because they had decided it was a dangerous error removing the "old landmarks" when it was not removing a peg of the old landmarks, but they had perverted ideas of what constituted the old landmarks. (MS 13. 1889, CWE 30; emphasis added).

There is very good reason why Ellen White so often compared this reaction against the 1888 message to the hatred of the Jews for Christ. The Jews were unconscious of their true motives; and our brethren were the same. Both the Jewish leaders and our brethren did not know that they were condemning "the greatest Teacher that the world ever knew." The unconscious nature of their sin is further disclosed as follows:

> I can never forget the experience which we had in Minneapolis, or the things which were then revealed to me in regard to the spirit that controlled men, the words spoken, the actions done in obedience to the powers of evil … They were moved at the meeting by another spirit, and *they knew not* that God had sent these young men to bear a special message to them which they treated with ridicule and contempt, not realizing that the heavenly intelligences

were looking upon them. *I know that at that time the Spirit of God was insulted.* (MS 24, 1892).

Is that sin still unrealized by us? Look at all the authoritative books published about our history during the past eight decades. Is there one that makes clear the full truth about 1888 and the beginning of the latter rain and the loud cry?

The following seems prophetic:

> The message of the True Witness finds the people of God in sad deception, yet honest in that deception. They know not that their condition is deplorable in the sight of God. (3T 253).

What we do find in our histories is much boasting of the marvelous "enrichment" that came to the Seventh-day Adventist Church in the 1888 message. We are "rich and increased with goods" is the general theme. Millions of our people around the world are ignorant of the sober fact that the Lord faithfully did His part and gave the "beginning" of the latter rain and the loud cry almost a century ago, but that the heavenly gift was rejected. The truth is as follows:

> Satan succeeded in shutting away from our people in a great measure, the special power of the Holy Spirit that God longed to impart to them.. The light that is to lighten the whole earth with its glory was resisted, and by the action of our own [leading] brethren has been in a great degree kept away from the world. (1SM 234, 235).

There is need for a final atonement or reconciliation with Christ in consequence of the "disgraceful treatment" accorded Him at one of our General Conference Sessions! This is *one* reason for it.

Indeed, the truth as found in the messages of Ellen G. White is "a startling denunciation" (3T 253), one that we could wish could be covered up forever or somehow successfully denied.

But the actual words of Christ in the Laodicean message pinpoint our self-imposed deception as basically *historical* in nature. The Greek expression is a very unusual one in that it repeats the same word "rich" in the clause, but in a different tense and voice. It puts in our lips the expression of a proud boast, "I am rich (in understanding righteousness by faith) because I have in my history been blessed by the acceptance of a great enrichment" (*plousios eimi, kai peplouteka*). Neither the King James translators or others were able to sense the full import of what they were seeking to translate from the Greek of the words of Jesus. Hence the King James translators tried to avoid what they thought was a meaningless repetition by a euphemism, "I am rich and increased with goods." This is understandable, for they lived too early. Consider the literal Greek of Revelation 3:17: "Thou sayest, Rich I am, and *I have been enriched*."

For decades we have shown a general feeling of satisfaction that we have been enriched by "glorious victory" in our 1888 history. Most of our ministers have been as sure that they understand and preach genuine righteousness by faith as that they understand and preach the Sabbath truth. Note how these various authors of our histories unwittingly confirm our Lord's charge, some even using the exact words that He has put into our lips:

> Higher achievement [1888] ... resulted in a spiritual awakening among our people. (M.E. Kern, R&H, Aug. 3, 1950, p. 294).

> A notable landmark in Seventh-day Adventist history ... crossing a continental divide into a new country ... a glorious victory ... a great spiritual awakening among Adventists. ... The dawn of a glorious day for the Adventist church. ... The blessed consequences of a great awakening ... are with us yet. ... This blessed period of revival beginning in 1888 ... was rich in both holiness and mission fruitage. (L.H.

Christian, *Fruitage of Spiritual Gifts*, pp. 219-245 — note the word "rich").

An inspiring message which rescued the church from the danger of legalism, and opened minds to the sublime reaches of the gospel. The last decade of the century saw the church developing, through this gospel, into a company prepared to fulfill the mission of God ... The church ... was aroused by the revived message of justification by faith. (A.W. Spalding, *Captains of the Host*, p. 602).

In many cases, churches that have begun with a profound evangelical emphasis have lost somewhat of their glow with the passing years. ... Seventh-day Adventism presents an interesting variation from the usual trend among religious bodies. ... Adventist history shows a growing emphasis upon evangelical truths. ... A religious denomination becoming more evangelical with the passing years is a unique phenomenon. (N.F. Pease, *By Faith Alone*, p. 227).

Foremost among such persons are those of a critical turn of mind who see only the failures of the church, but who are blind to its achievements. While we regret our neglect of the great truths of the gospel, we thank God for the noble men and women who have emphasized these truths through the years. We also salute the unnumbered army of church members who know Christ as a personal Saviour, and who have been truly justified by faith alone. We are grateful for the crescendo of emphasis on justification by faith during the past forty years; and while we have not done all we should or might have done, we are unwise to ignore the progress that has been made. (*Ibid.*, p. 238).

During my fifty-five years in the Seventh-day Adventist ministry I have come in contact with our workers and members all around the world. I have associated with our ministers in nearly every land where our work is established ... I have never heard a worker or a lay member — in

America, Europe or anywhere else — express opposition to the message of righteousness by faith. (A.V. Olson, *Through Crisis to Victory, 1888-1901*, p. 232; *Thirteen Years of Crisis* (1982), p. 238).

It is correct to say that the message [of righteousness by faith] has been declared, both from the pulpit and through the press, and by the lives of thousands upon thousands of Gods dedicated people who have learned the result of spiritual life in Christ. Anyone who takes the time to examine Seventh-day Adventist books, papers, pamphlets, and tracts will discover that this glorious truth has been printed time and time again.. The various phases of salvation through faith in Christ have been taught with power and clarity over the radio for a number of years and more recently on television. This subject has been made prominent in different courses of Bible correspondence lessons. Adventist pastors and evangelists have announced this vital truth from church pulpits and public platforms, with hearts aflame with love for Christ. (*Ibid.*, pp. 233- 237; new edition, pp. 239-243).

This chapter can only touch the tremendous emphasis on justification by faith at the General Conference of 1926. It is my firm opinion that it would be well to give less emphasis to 1888 and more emphasis to 1926. ... Some have suggested that the denomination should go on record in some specific way, acknowledging the mistakes of 1888. No more positive evidence of spiritual growth and maturity could be presented than the sermons of 1926. (N.F. Pease, *The Faith That Saves*, p. 59).

"Thou sayest, Rich I am, and I have been enriched!" 1888 was the beginning of a great enrichment, a glorious victory, "spiritual ... maturity." We are unique. We are getting better and better.

These historians were all earnest, dedicated, faithful men. They sincerely tried to reflect a common pride and satisfaction in the tremendous "progress" of the church. But not one has been able to recognize the import of the Laodicean message, that it is precisely in our assumed "enrichment" through acceptance of righteousness by faith that we are self-deceived. Not one recognizes the need for a reconciliation with Christ through a final atonement in consequence of the disgraceful treatment accorded Him at one of our General Conference Sessions. They all seek to find better words to describe our present spiritual state than the inspired one, "deplorable."

Not one has discerned that in 1926 and currently our boasted "spiritual growth and maturity" in understanding and proclaiming "righteousness by faith" was not in the acceptance of the 1888 message, but in accepting the popular Protestant, Evangelical, or Calvinist message of justification and righteousness by faith. They have mistakenly assumed that this "unique phenomenon" of the Seventh-day Adventist church becoming more "evangelical" was through acceptance of the message that was to have been the beginning of the Latter Rain and the Loud Cry. Instead, we have unwittingly gotten away from that message that the Lord gave us, and have adopted views almost identical to those who reject the three angels' messages. And we are pleased with this "profound evangelical emphasis," sadly unaware that it is not the true "everlasting gospel."

This is the true remnant church, and its future is indeed bright. The work will triumph. And the Lord has blessed. And He will bless. But the point is that His version of the significance of our denominational history is much safer for us to follow than that opposed to it. The Laodicean message is still "present truth." The Lord says we are in reality "wretched, and miserable, and poor, and blind, and naked". The great victory of the Church is still future and lies on the other side of accepting the divinely recommended remedy for our present condition — repentance.

There is something that we can do and that is to do exactly what our Lord says:

> I counsel thee to buy of Me gold tried in the fire, that thou mayest be rich; and white raiment that thou mayest be clothed, and that the shame of thy nakedness do not appear, and anoint thine eyes with eyesalve, that thou mayest see. As many as I love, I rebuke and chasten: be zealous therefore, and repent (Rev. 3:18, 19).

Of all our official histories, the most pronounced — yet still unconscious — denial of our Lords message was published in 1966. Utterly sincere and most earnest and devoted, the author was desirous of defending the "angel of the church of the Laodiceans." After his death, his publishers entitled his book *Through Crisis to Victory, 1888-1901*. Thus they clearly advanced the novel thesis that the 1901 General Conference Session undid the 1888 opposition to the message of Christ's righteousness with all its attendant organizational evils, and ushered in "victory."

This prestigious work has made a profound impression on the world church. Any Ellen G. White statements that contradict the basic thesis of the book are naturally assumed to be suspect. "What they say in plain English cannot be true if this authoritative book says the opposite. Some mysterious context must cancel out the import of any statements that say that the 1901 Session was not 'victory.'" So readers are understandably inclined to assume. (It is significant that the book has been re-published officially in 1981 under a new title, but with its "rich and increased with goods" thesis still intact, assuming that the 1901 Conference ended the "crisis" years in virtual "victory.")

Nevertheless, the clear facts indicate that the results of the 1901 Session did not undo the tragic unbelief manifested at the 1888 Session. A number of Ellen G. White statements are consistent and emphatic:

What a wonderful work could have been done for the vast company gathered in Battle Creek at the General Conference [of 1901], if the leaders of our work had taken themselves in hand. But the work that all heaven was waiting to do as soon as men prepared the way, was not done; for the leaders closed and bolted the door against the Spirit's entrance. There was a stopping short of entire surrender to God. And hearts that might have been purified from all error were strengthened in wrong doing The doors were barred against the heavenly current that would have swept away all evil. Men left their sins unconfessed. (Letter to Dr. J.H. Kellogg, Aug. 5, 1902).

The result of the last General Conference has been the greatest, the most terrible sorrow of my life. No change was made. The spirit that should have been brought into the whole work as the result of that meeting was not brought in because men did not receive the testimonies of the Spirit of God. As they went to their several fields of labor, they did not walk in the light that the Lord had flashed upon their pathway, but carried into their work the wrong principles that had been prevailing in the work at Battle Creek. ... It is a perilous thing to reject the light that God sends. (Letter to Judge Jesse Arthur, Jan. 15, 1903).

If the men who heard the message given at the time of the Conference — the most solemn message that could be given — had not been so unimpressionable, if in sincerity they had asked, "Lord, what wilt Thou have me to do?" the experience of the past year would have been very different from what it is. But they have not made the track clean behind them. They have not confessed their mistakes, and now they are going over the same ground in many things, following the same wrong course of action, because they have destroyed their spiritual eyesight ...

If the work begun at the General Conference had been carried forward to perfection, I should not be called upon to write these words. There was opportunity to confess or deny wrong, and in many cases the denial came, to avoid the consequence of confession.

Unless there is a reformation, calamity will overtake the publishing house, and the world will know the reason. I have been shown that there has not been a turning to God with full purpose of heart. ... God has been mocked by your hardness of heart, which is continually increasing. (*Testimonies*, Vol. 7, pp. 93-96. "read to the Review and Herald Board in November, 1901." The next testimony beginning on page 97 is entitled, "The Review and Herald Fire").

As regards the 1888 message of Christ's righteousness, it must be hailed as "victory" even though the "works" that followed the assumed "faith" led to the divine rebuke in the disastrous fires that destroyed our Sanitarium and publishing house in Battle Creek, clearly a rebuke from the Lord.

In the 1901 meeting the committee members elected at that time were, as far as we can discover, men who fully believed in this doctrine [of righteousness by faith], though some may not have entered fully into the personal experience of surrender and faith. ... I have attended Adventist camp meetings, annual meetings, conference and mission sessions, workers' meetings, and other gatherings, and I can truthfully say that in all this association with church workers and people of different races, nations and tongues during my fifty-five years in the Seventh-day Adventist ministry, I have never heard a worker or a lay member- in America, Europe, or anywhere else — express opposition to the message of righteousness by faith. Neither have I known of any such opposition having been expressed by Seventh-day Adventist publications. (A.V. Olson, *Through Crisis to Victory 1888-1901*, pp. 228-232: new edition, pp. 234-238).

But our author was earnest and sincere and deeply spiritual. Something was wrong, he clearly knew. The work was years behind and the coming of the Lord was long delayed. This he could not and would not deny. He frankly recognized the problem and advanced his own sincere conviction as to why the church as a whole did not at this late date understand and receive the truth of righteousness by faith so the world work could be finished. Seldom has an official writer so graphically yet unconsciously confirmed the truth of our Lords diagnosis in His message to "the angel" of the Laodicean church, or so earnestly and sincerely insisted that "the angel" is "rich and increased with goods." The ministerial spokesmen for the church are rich, the author maintains, in understanding and proclaiming the message. He recognizes no need on their part, and lays the blame for the unfinished task rather on the obtuse laity. *They* are the ones who are "wretched, miserable, poor, and blind, and naked."

Note the very clear import of the conclusion of the book:

Through the years since 1901 and before, Seventh-day Adventists have published numerous tracts on righteousness by faith, and from time to time this theme has been covered in Sabbath School lessons. The various phases of salvation through faith in Christ have been taught with power and clarity over the radio for a number of years and more recently on television. This subject has been made prominent in different courses of Bible correspondence lessons. Adventist pastors and evangelists have announced this vital truth from church pulpits and public platforms, with hearts aflame with love for Christ And through the monthly journal, *The Ministry*, Seventh-day Adventist preachers and writers have constantly been urged to make Jesus Christ and His righteousness as the Saviour the center of all their teaching.

This emphasis has not been more prominent than the importance of the subject merits. If anything, it has not been so great as this precious theme deserves. (*Ibid.*, p. 237; new edition, p. 243).

Then why hasn't the work been finished if this precious truth has been so "taught with power and clarity ... with hearts aflame" by Adventist pastors and evangelists? The lay members haven't listened as they should, The latter have held up the finishing of the work Note the conclusion, possible only through a misunderstanding of the Laodicean message:

> Many Seventh-day Adventists still seem ignorant of this all-important doctrine. Much of this lack of awareness results from their failure to read Adventist books and periodicals presenting the gospel in clear, forceful language ...
>
> We fear that to many church members the message of righteousness by faith has become a dry theory instead of a living reality in their daily experience.
>
> They have neglected the light that God in His love and mercy has caused to shine upon them They have failed to exchange the worthless garments of their own self-righteousness for the spotless robe of Christ's righteousness. In the sight of God their poor souls are naked and destitute. (*Ibid.*, pp. 237-239; new edition, pp. 243-247).

If our Lord's message is true, here we have the cart before the horse. Our Lord addresses His message "unto *the angel* of the church." The emphasis in the Spirit of Prophecy is crystal clear: had the ministerial leadership of the church truly accepted the 1888 message, the church would have cooperated and the work would have been finished (cf. 1SM 234, 235). "Thy people shall be willing in the day of Thy power," the Psalmist assures us (Ps. 110:3). A laity continually resisting leadership is a discouraging prospect for the future! It is not true.

What our author cannot see is that all this "emphasis" he finds so encouraging is in reality a different message from the 1888 message, and this is the reason "the message of righteousness by faith has become a dry theory" " to many church members." They are bored by it so that there is a "lack of awareness ... from their failure to read Adventist books and periodicals." Surely they have tried to read them; but the clear, cogent concepts of the 1888 message being lacking, the message seems dull to them. And they don't know why. But "the angel of the church" feels he has done his duty, at least quite largely so and commendably so.

What is said here is said with deep respect for all our historians, whose devotion to the cause was unquestionable. The "thou knowest not" of our Lord explains the problem. And they merely articulate the nearly universal pride of many who still uphold this view in the matter of righteousness by faith (cf. *Movement of Destiny*, pp. 610-612). Nothing said here is to be understood as critical of any of our past writers. It is said simply from the realization that our Lord's message in Revelation 3:14-21 is still "present truth," and clearly demonstrated to be so from our own denominational history, past and current.

In this recent work (republished 1978) practically every prominent spokesman for the church is quoted as supporting the theme of 1888 "enrichment" (a few are notably absent, such as S.N. Haskell, Meade MacGuire, and Taylor G. Bunch). The list of names quoted (pp. 681-686, 1971 ed.) is very impressive indeed. If truth can be settled by a majority vote, then it seems certain that Ellen White was sadly mistaken in her repeated statements to the effect that the 1888 message was "in a great measure" and "in a great degree" "shut away from our people" and "kept away from the world" "by the action of our own [leading] brethren." Not one of these dedicated men cited would want to contradict the True Witness knowingly. But could it be that our Lord's words "thou knowest not" apply to all of us?

The simple fact of the inexplicable passage of time for nearly a century beyond the "beginning" of the latter rain forces us to reconsider the significance of our history. If the latter rain was accepted so eagerly and faithfully by our forefathers, why wasn't the work of God finished in their generation? Ellen White's testimony is so simple that even a child can grasp it: true acceptance of the message would have meant the finishing of the gospel commission and the return of our Lord in that generation.

The repeated affirmation of the "angel," "Rich I am and I have been enriched," is bound to have a deep influence on our world-wide church. Deep-rooted but subtle pride hardens the heart Repeated, widespread affirmations of "enrichment" prejudice hearts against our Lords Laodicean message when it is understood in its true import Resentment arises against His appeal to "repent" as a church. "Have we not been told for many decades that we are 'rich in understanding righteousness by faith? Why this devastating charge that we are 'wretched, miserable, poor, blind and naked'?" And many are offended. The ultimate shaking would never be so terrible had not Christ's message been so repeatedly contradicted.

Scripture is replete with prophecies of world wide dissemination of pure gospel truth. "The earth shall be filled with the knowledge of the glory of the Lord, as the waters cover the sea" (Hab. 2:14). "Living waters shall go out from Jerusalem" (Zech. 14:8). "Arise, shine; for thy light is come, and the glory of the Lord is risen upon thee. For, behold, the darkness shall cover the earth, and gross darkness the people: but the Lord shall arise upon thee, and His glory shall be seen upon thee. And the Gentiles shall come to thy light, and kings to the brightness of thy rising" (Isa. 60:1-3). "It shall come to pass in the last days, saith God, I will pour out of My Spirit upon all flesh: and your sons and your daughters shall prophesy, and your young men shall see visions, and your old men shall dream dreams: and on My servants and on My handmaidens I will pour out in those days of My Spirit" (Acts 2:17, 18). "I saw another angel come down from heaven, having great power: and the earth was lightened with His glory." (Rev. 18:1).

Is there anyone concerned that our campaigns and publications are not as yet truly fulfilling these prophecies? Can it honestly be said that our message is stirring the world, or even arousing any significant opposition as in apostolic times?

Is it more expensive slick paper that our publications need? More four-color pictures, more refinement of the photoengraver's art? Is it merely more money, more psychology, more music, more professional finesse, that our evangelistic campaigns need?

Or is there a problem with the message content, the proclamation of gospel truth itself! Our Lord says we are "poor," where we have thought we are "rich," in our comprehension and proclamation of "the third angel's message in verity," the pure truth of the gospel that has not been clearly seen "since the day of Pentecost." (FCE 473).

It is an old cliché with us to say that "we need the Holy Spirit." Of course, we do; but the reception and inspiration of the Holy spirit is not a matter of magic or good fortune. "The gospel of Christ ... is the power of God unto salvation" (Rom. 1:16), and that "power" is not resident in emotional extravaganza but in *truth*, even "the truth of the gospel." (Gal. 2:14).

"We have the truth," is the universal boast. The music on the record is fine; all we might need perhaps is a little more "emphasis," to turn up the volume control a little. Many who speak of righteousness by faith speak of it as a proud possession and our proclamation of it as solely a matter of "emphasis," of how much the volume control needs to be turned up from time to time.

But gospel truth has nothing to do with such "emphasis." The very use of the word betrays an ignorance of what it is. Who would dare say that the apostles preached a mere "re-emphasis" of Judaism? Nowhere did Ellen White use the word "emphasis" or "re-emphasis" in relation to the 1888 message of Christ's righteousness, as though it were a matter of mere adjustment of homiletic balance. Righteousness by faith is a vital, throbbing, explosive truth, and God has given man no volume-control knob to "emphasize" it with, to turn it up or down. You have it or you don't have it; and if you have it, you turn the world upside down. Nothing less.

And if we're not turning the world upside down, the only thing to do is to confess that the True Witness is right. We *are* wretched and poor, whereas we have pathetically thought we are rich. Until the "angel" sees it and confesses it, there can be no will to take the proffered remedies the True Witness has for us.

Our "poverty" is painfully evident in an erosion of confidence in the one unique Seventh-day Adventist doctrine — the cleansing of the sanctuary that began in 1844. Verdict Publications is publishing reports that:

> leading Adventist scholars ... now think that the distinctive Adventist doctrine of the investigative judgment is not demonstrable from the Bible. ... Other scholars ... have quietly abandoned belief in this teaching [the 1844 doctrine]. We could easily mention the chairmen of theology departments and other prominent scholars who have lost faith in this distinctive Adventist doctrine. ... This loss of faith in 1844 has taken place. ... There is a widespread feeling that our case for 1844 and our explanation of it are no longer convincing or perhaps no longer viable. A large percentage of Adventists in Europe have long considered

1844 as a peculiar American aberration. (*1844 Re-examined,* pp. 9, 10).

Numerous pastors and theologians are cited as favoring this basic questioning of basic Adventist roots. Yet the original research of Crosier, Edson, and Hahn in formulating the distinctive Adventist concept of the cleansing of the sanctuary was thoroughly Biblical. It was this that established our existence as a people. If it is not authentically Biblical, Seventh-day Adventists have no real theological reason to exist. If the "dragon" who is "wroth with the woman" wants to destroy her, could he do so more effectively than to lunge at her jugular vein?

The virtual eclipse of the 1888 message for decades has been the one factor almost entirely responsible for this erosion of basic Seventh-day Adventist confidence in the sanctuary doctrine and 1844. In 1889 Ellen White foresaw that opposition to the Jones-Waggoner message was "to cause apostasy" (CWE 31). An interesting phenomenon is apparent: those who fail to see Biblical support for 1844 likewise fail to appreciate the 1888 message; and the reverse seems operative as well. The 1888 message brought the sanctuary doctrine into clear focus and restored "its presiding power [in] the hearts of believers" (EV 225); and the loss of that message tended to "remove its presiding power from the hearts of believers."

7

The Divinely Appointed Remedies: "Gold"

Our Lord counsels us to "buy of Me gold tried in the fire, that thou mayest be rich" (Revelation 3:18). We all know that the "gold tried in the fire is faith that works by love." (COL 158).

If we already possessed the "gold', we would not be urged to "buy" it. We must cease assuming that we already possess it and need only more efficient methods of displaying it — more modern methods of journalism, more money for TV and radio stations, or better techniques of homiletics. Our need is basic. In respect of the very "gold" itself, the True Witness says our treasure-box is empty. Christ Himself says so.

It is quite possible that once we "buy" the gold itself so that we actually do possess it, we will not be so distraught in our search for adequate means to display it. Perhaps the Lord of hosts who says, "The silver is Mine, and the gold is Mine," will then convict generous hearts to give prodigally for the world-wide display of His people's "gold" when that time comes.

It is the "angel" who is counseled by the True Witness, not just "some" individuals here and there. It is the general body of the church leadership. There is no way that we can evade the direct point of his "counsel." All attempts to evade it will only result in more confusion and postponing the finishing of Gods work for further decades. Heaven pity us if we remonstrate with our Lord and insist, "But I have always understood the gospel and taught it with power! I know *I* understand it. Thou canst not mean *me!* Thou hast blessed *my* work so wonderfully. 'We have eaten and drunk in Thy presence, and Thou has taught in our streets!' 'Lord, Lord, have we not prophesied in Thy name? and in Thy name have cast out devils? and in Thy name have done many wonderful works?'" (Matt. 7:22; Luke 14:26).

Our Lord says to the lukewarm "angel" in this time of such immense eschatological opportunity, "I feel like vomiting you out of My mouth (*mello se emesai*)" (Rev. 3:16). This warning is parallel to that Christ gives those who say, "Lord, Lord, open unto us; ... I tell you, I know you not whence ye are; depart from Me, all ye workers of iniquity. There shall be weeping and gnashing of teeth" (Luke 13:25-28). That's an awful word — "iniquity." We instinctively pass it on to our non-believing neighbors. What we need to realize is that Christian experience perfectly acceptable in times previous to the cleansing of the sanctuary becomes "lukewarmness" in our day. Measured devotion appropriate during the ministry of the High Priest in the Holy Apartment becomes "iniquity" when weighed against the incomparably greater scope of consecration appropriate to His ministry in the most Holy Apartment. (See Leviticus 23:27-32).

To our High Priest, there is no more nauseating sin than this. And still it is not "works" that He is talking about. The "gold" we lack is not more feverish activity. That we are truly "rich" in already. It is faith, pure and true, that we must "buy."

Why "buy" it? Why doesn't He say, "Ask of Me, and I will *give* it to you"? Could it be that we must surrender our false concepts of faith in exchange for the true? The Laodicean message recognizes that we are in possession of some kind of tender that must be exchanged at the heavenly commissary for the "gold," like one barters for an object to be bought. The counsel to "buy" is very significant. Note what "goods" we do possess:

> Because thou sayest, I am rich and increased with goods. (Rev. 3:17).

What greater deception can come upon human minds than a confidence that they are right, when they are all wrong! The message of the True Witness finds the people of God in a sad deception, yet honest in that deception ... Those addressed are flattering themselves that they are in an exalted spiritual condition ... secure in their attainments ... *rich in spiritual knowledge.*"(3T 252-253. emphasis added).

The "price" we must give up is "deception," false "spiritual knowledge." In other words, we must surrender our false ideas and mistaken conceptions in order to "buy" the "gold." Let us look again at the inspired definition of the "gold" that we need:

That the trial of your faith, being much more precious than of gold that perisheth, though it be tried with fire, might be found unto praise and honour and glory at the appearing of Jesus Christ. (1Pet 1:7).

The gold tried in the tire is faith that works by love. Only this can bring us into harmony with God. We may be active, we may do much work; but without love, *such love as dwelt in the heart of Christ*, we can never be numbered with the family of heaven. (COL 158, emphasis added).

The gold here recommended as having being tried in the fire, is faith and love. It makes the heart rich; for it has been purged until it is pure, and the more it is tested the more brilliant is its luster. (4T 88).

We have been talking about "faith and love" for many decades. Don't we have them by now? What meaning is there here? Can we gloss this over with a few pious platitudes? Or is our Lord trying to tell us that we don't really understand what love is, and therefore cannot have true faith? Is the "angel" of the Church destitute of "such love as dwelt in the heart of Christ"?

Yes, he is, according to the True Witness. This is very shocking to contemplate. But let us look more deeply into the matter. There are two great antithetical ideas of "love." One has come from Hellenism and is the kind of "love" on which popular evangelical Christianity is based. The other is completely different, and is the kind of love that can have its source only in the ministry of the true High Priest in His cleansing of the heavenly sanctuary. (EW 55, 56).

Our Lords charge becomes baffling and incomprehensible to us when we are ignorant of what that love really is. "Love — why, that's the very thing I'm strong on! I know I love my loved ones and my brethren. What lack I yet?" Self-satisfied hearts will feel no need and probably at this late hour cannot be awakened. But many do indeed feel a great need and will immediately recognize the "gold" when they see it.

Remember that in its full context, the inspired pen says the "gold' is "faith that works by love." Therefore, in order to understand what the True Witness means by saying "buy of Me gold tried in the fire," we must first of all examine what "love" is. Only then will we be able to understand what "faith" is.

Christ Himself makes clear what New Testament faith is, and His view is different from that of the popular concept. "For God so loved the world that He gave His only begotten Son, that whosoever believeth in Him ..." (John 3:16). Note: (1) Gods love is the first thing, and until that love is revealed there can be no "believing." (2) As the result of His "loving" and "giving," the sinner finds it possible to "believe." ("To believe" and "to have faith" is one word in Greek). Thus, faith is a heart-experience, "heart-work" to borrow Ellen White's phrase, and it cannot exist until God's love is understood and appreciated.

Please note very carefully a fundamental point: the "believing" is not motivated by a fear of perishing or an acquisitive reward of everlasting life. The primary causative clause of Jesus' statement is "for God so *loved*." The two secondary clauses are "that He *gave* His only begotten Son" and "that whosoever *be-*

lieveth." The believing is a direct result of the loving. And Christ Himself spoke the words of John 3:16.

Thus there begins to emerge a clear definition of New Testament "faith": *Faith is a heart-response to, or a heart-appreciation of: the love of God revealed at the cross.* Re-read Romans and Galatians with this John 3:16 definition in mind and you will find Paul reproduced with startling high-fidelity realism. He will come alive for you.

The redemption from perishing and the reward of everlasting life are only by-products of genuine New Testament faith. The twin motivations of fear-of-hell and hope-of-reward are not valid aspects of the faith itself.

There are those who are perplexed by this New Testament definition of faith. They feel inclined to accept the idea that Ellen G. White has somehow changed Christ's and Paul's definition of faith and made it a self-centered acquisitive act of the soul as the popular churches teach. In her writings, they say, faith is "trust," and "trust" presupposes a state of egocentric insecurity. It is true that she often says that faith is trust. In fact there are scores of differing definitions of faith in the *Index* among the 700 entries under that word. There were probably many varying nuances of meaning even in Paul's day.

But Ellen White does not destroy Paul's grand concept of faith. When the apostle presented his great teaching of "righteousness by faith," the word "faith" gained a stupendous, explicit and dynamic meaning that was not possible before the cross or at least could not be clearly seen until then. Even Nicodemus, who heard Jesus say the words in John 3:16, could not see it until the cross. Hellenistic Greek cannot define faith clearly.

It was the same with the word "love." No one really knew what love was until the cross. The life and death of Jesus invested an obscure Greek word, *agape*, with a meaning never dreamed of before. And then these two words, *agape*, and its human response, faith, turned the ancient "world upside down." And Ellen G. White is in complete harmony with New Testament faith.

We understand neither Paul or Ellen White until we recognize that the faith which brings righteousness is something immeasurably greater than the egocentric idea we have supposed it to be. The only entry among the 700 in the *Index* that is the common denominator of them all is the same as Paul's working definition of faith: "Faith — Genuine (or real) always works by love" (6BC 1111; *Index*, Vol. 1, p. 968). Note how she clearly upholds Paul's definition of faith:

> Joshua desired to lead them to serve God, not by compulsion, but willingly. Love to God is the very foundation of religion. To engage in His service merely from hope of reward or fear of punishment would avail nothing. Open apostasy would not be more offensive to God than hypocrisy and mere formal worship. (PP 523).

> It is not the fear of punishment or the hope of everlasting reward that leads the disciples of Christ to follow Him. They behold the Saviour's matchless love, revealed throughout His pilgrimage on earth, from the manger of Bethlehem to Calvary's cross, and the sight of Him attracts, it softens and subdues the soul. Love awakens in the heart of the beholders. They hear His voice, and they follow him. (DA 480).

> There are those who profess to serve God, while they rely upon their own efforts to obey His law, to form a right character and secure salvation. Their hearts are not moved by any deep sense of the love of Christ, but they seek to perform the duties of the Christian life as that which God requires of them in order to gain heaven. *Such religion is worth nothing.* (SC 44, 45, emphasis added).

The context of the last statement is interesting. With the strongest emphasis that words could possibly convey, Ellen White continually points us to the cross and the revelation of Gods love there. This is the true motivation for serving the Lord, she says. And of this motivation she adds:

> Oh, let us contemplate the amazing sacrifice that has been made for us! Let us try to appreciate the labor and energy that Heaven is expending to reclaim the lost, and bring them back to the Father's house. Motives stronger, and agencies more powerful, could never be brought into operation; ... Let us place ourselves in right relation to Him who has loved us with amazing love. (SC 21, 22).

It is true that the Lords messenger also employs other "mighty incentives and encouragements to urge us to give the heart's loving service to our Creator and Redeemer," which appear superficially to endorse a self-centered view of faith. This is perplexing. Does she contradict herself? Are we to remain in a kind of limbo on this matter, and when we read of the love of God revealed at the cross tend to discount it as ineffective motivation?

Four possible explanations of these apparent contradictions are:

1. "The worlds Redeemer accepts men as they are, with all their wants, imperfections, and weaknesses" (SC 46), and lets them begin the Christian life with whatever motivation they are at the moment capable of. Many may be baptized from purely selfish reasons with no appreciation of Calvary. Their religion is at present "worth nothing" (SC 45), but at least the law is their "schoolmaster" to bring them unto Christ that eventually they "might be justified by faith" (Gal. 3:24).

2. Millions of Christians have gone into the grave without ever properly appreciating the Atonement. They lived in eras

of comparative darkness, and lived up to all the light they had. They never found full release from self-centered legalism, but they did the best they could. The Lord has accepted them. Many of them have died since *Steps to Christ* was published. There is help in that book for those who prepare for death. But there is also help there for those who will prepare for translation!

3. The work of the High Priest in the Most Holy Apartment will result in the complete purification of the motives of those who follow His work by faith. They will become mature Christians and "put away childish things" (1 Cor. 13:11). In the full context of Paul's chapter on *agape*, "childish things" are self-centered motivations. By understanding that Ellen White ministered in a transition period, her apparent contradictions are resolved. Not yet had all of God's people been ready to "put away childish things," nor were they quite ready yet to know that motivation "which is perfect."

4. With no desire to contradict what our Lord says, it may be better to be a "lukewarm" church member than not to be a member at all. At least this is what we have supposed for many decades, hence many immature efforts to increase our membership. If a person accepts the terms of church membership and enters the church, however unconscious he may be of his true spiritual state, there is always a chance that he will respond to the Holy Spirit and overcome his lukewarmness.

When our Lord says, "I would thou wert cold or hot," we may not necessarily assume He means He wishes we were either "hot" members or completely out of the church. Perhaps so; but He may mean He wishes we were either "hot" members, or "cold" members who truly felt our need of warmth. The popular self-centered motivations employed in some evangelism may indeed increase our membership; the point is, the true "constraint" of the love of Christ alone can enable us to overcome our lukewarmness.

Before we turn to examine more closely what New Testament love is, let us look at one more Ellen G. White statement that is exceedingly clear and incisive on this matter of faith being a heart-appreciation of the Atonement:

> The precious blood of Jesus is the fountain prepared to cleanse the soul from the defilement of sin. When you determine to take Him as your friend, a new and enduring light will shine from the cross of Christ. A true sense of the sacrifice and intercession of the dear Saviour will break the heart that has become hardened in sin; and love, thankfulness, and humility will come into the soul. The surrender of the heart to Jesus subdues the rebel into a penitent, and then the language of the obedient soul is, "Old things are passed away; behold, all things are become new." This is the true religion of the Bible. Everything short of this is a deception. (4T 625).

Neither the words "faith" nor "righteousness" appear in this passage; yet righteousness is certainly the experience described. If righteousness comes only by faith, it becomes obvious that true faith must be the means that effects this great change.

Returning to our topic of the "gold" we are counseled to "buy," we must seek to discover what New Testament love is. Unless we understand and appreciate that, we cannot possibly understand what faith is. Very briefly we may summarize the contrast between Gods heavenly love (*agape*) and the human emotion we all know which is commonly assumed to be "love":

The Common Idea of Love	God's Love (Agape)
1. Always dependent on beauty or goodness of its object Loves "its own," such as family or those who are good to us.	1. Loves those who are ugly or unworthy. "God commendeth His *agape* toward us, in that while we were yet sinners [and enemies] Christ died for us" (Romans 5:8, 10).
2. Rests on a sense of need, as husband or wife loves spouse because of need, or children love parents, and parents their children, because they need them.	2. God, who is infinite in wealth, loves out of His goodness alone. "He [Christ] was rich, yet for your sakes He became poor" (2 Cor. 8:9).
3. Dependent on value of its object.	3. Creates value in its object (Isa. 13:12).
4. Man seeking after God. All false religion based on idea that God is esoteric, hiding Himself. Salvation thus depends on man's initiative.	4. Not man seeking God but God seeking after man. "The Son of man is come to seek and to save …" (Luke 19:10). Thus, salvation dependent on Gods initiative, not ours.
5. Always aspires to climb up higher. Continual motivation of sinful man. (Seen even in the church and ministerial leadership).	5. Ready to step down lower. Purest revelation of *agape* seen in Philippians 2:5-8. Christ was in highest place but stepped down to lowest, "even the death of the cross."
6. Is basically self-love. Modern evangelical leaders now strongly teach necessity for primary love of self. Self-love confused with proper sense of self-respect dependent on appreciation of Christ's sacrifice in our behalf. Ultimate dimension of self-love:	6. Is the utter emptying of self. (But this is not monastic asceticism or egocentric self-denial pursued as a means to a greater eventual reward. Such is mere religious opportunism). "Seeketh not her own," genuinely seeks the good of others. Its fullest dimension is the following:

7. Desires immortality as heavenly reward. All religions, Christian or non-Christian, appeal to this basic egocentric motivation. Has been dominant motivation employed in much Seventh-day Adventist evangelism. Responsible for egocentric lukewarmness.	7. Willing to sacrifice eternal life, even to be lost eternally. Supreme demonstration is Christ on His cross where He died the equivalent of the "second death" for us. Moses and Paul are examples of redeemed sinners who knew such *agape* (cf. Ex. 32:32; Rom. 9:1-3).

(Contrasts adapted from Anders Nygren, *Agape and Eros*, p. 210).

These contrasts explain why John created that sublime equation "God is *agape*." And "he that loveth not [with *agape*] knoweth not God," but "every one that loveth [with *agape*] is born of God, and knoweth God. ... Herein is our agape made perfect, that we may have boldness in the day of judgment. ... There is no fear in agape; but perfect *agape* casteth out fear. ... He that feareth is not made perfect in *agape*." No one can invent or originate such love from a human source! "We love because He first loved us" (1 John 4:7-19).

This was the idea that turned the ancient world upside down in the time of the apostles (Acts 17:6). It will turn the world upside down again when the remnant church comprehends "with all saints what is the breadth, and length, and depth, and height ... to know the *agape* of Christ, which passeth knowledge (Eph. 3:17-19). Without such *agape*, all our "tongues of men and of angels" are "as sounding brass, or a tinkling cymbal"; all our prophecy, "knowledge," and "faith ... to remove mountains" is nothing. So terrible is the self-deception we are prone to that we can "bestow all my goods to feed the poor ... and give my body to be burned" and yet lack the true motivation of *agape* (1Cor. 13:1-3). (This, incidentally, is Laodicean lukewarmness! It could continue for thousands of years and Gods work not be finished).

Whereas all non-Christian religions as well as apostate Christianity appeal to man's self-centeredness and insecurity, the apostles presented a gospel with a radically different appeal. Paul, for example, did not begin his preaching with a presentation of man's need, but of Gods deed. "When I came to you, ... I determined not to know anything among you, save Jesus Christ and Him crucified" (1 Cor. 2:1, 2). "I delivered unto you first of all that which I also received [first], how that Christ died for our sins" (1 Cor. 15:3). The result was the development of true faith in the hearts of the listeners. An example Paul mentions is the Galatians themselves, whose response was the "hearing of faith" (cf. Gal, 3:1, 2) a true heart-appreciation of that "wondrous cross, on which the Prince of glory died." Such a heart response is the true article of "faith" found in New Testament justification by faith. (This, incidentally, is the third angel's message *in verity!*).

This is why such justification by faith leads to "obedience to all the commandments of God" (TM 92) including willing acceptance of the Sabbath truth. "*Agape* is the fulfilling of the law." (Romans 13:10).

The true Christocentric motivation for service and obedience finds refreshing demonstration in the appeals of the 1888 messengers, in contrast to its almost total extinction in our day (thank God, it is beginning to appear again). A.T. Jones said:

> I heard of a person who made an expression something like this, speaking of the missionary work "Oh, I must do more work or I will not have stars in my crown. I must do more or someone else will have more stars than I." Fine motive, isn't it? The person who works for stars in his crown, that he may have more stars than somebody else will never have any stars at all. That is not the right motive; nothing is the right motive but love for Christ.

Think of it, my brethren, if I should be so happy and so glad as to get to that blessed place, and the Saviour should hand me a crown, do you think brethren, that I could stand in His presence and put it on? ... Do you think that I could stand before my master and beholding the print of the nails in His hand, and see the marks of the thorns that pierced His lovely brow, — do you think I say, that I could ... receive from those hands a crown, to be placed on my head? No! No! I would want to bow low at His knee and put it on His head, for His is the power and the glory. Let His be the eternal joy, and let mine be to see His glory, and I shall be satisfied.

I have thought but little of my crown; but I have thought that if I can add one beam of glory to His countenance, one ray of gladness to the brow that was pierced with thorns, that if I can add one glimmer of joy to that face, oh! ... then my joy will be complete. ... Let the love of Christ constrain us.

Brethren, if we keep our minds on Christ, we will not be troubled with thinking of the stars in our crown, for our salvation will be sure and our joy full. He wants us to work and oh, let us work from that motive of love. (Sermon, Sept. 24, 1888, Oakland, California; RG11 Presidential Documents, 1863-1901, Manuscripts & Typescripts folder, General Conference Archives).

It is painful for us moderns to contemplate the complete contrast in motive in this appeal with that which is so exceedingly popular in our day. We love to sing, "Will there be any stars in *my* crown?' (Many of our hymns and gospel songs are as far from New Testament religion as Augustine's theology which formed the basis of medieval piety). The above hymn was written in 1897 (*Church Hymnal* No. 626) and illustrates the falling away from New Testament agape that began with the early church and has never yet been properly faced and corrected.

Long before the true Sabbath was changed into Sunday, our Lord rebuked the "angel of the church of Ephesus," "I have somewhat against thee, because thou has left thy first love (*agape*)" (Rev. 2:4). We have superficially assumed that this was a sort of romantic backsliding, interpreting "first love" in terms of our own emotional experiences. But our Lord is not here discussing sentimentalism.

The one New Testament concept that Satan hates pre-eminently is *agape*, the very antithesis of his raison d'etre. It being the principle that effectively destroys his egocentric commitment, *agape* became his first target of attack in the early church. The writings of the "Fathers" document the truth of our Lords charge to "the angel of the church of Ephesus." Like termites stealthily burrowing from deep within, ideas from heathenism began finding entrance into the early church. First was the idea of self-centered love (*eros*) as an alternative to New Testament *agape*, in order to replace the true Christocentric motivation with an egocentric one. The change of the Sabbath into Sunday could never have found acceptance among early Christians had not the groundwork been previously laid by the adulteration of the true concept of love.

Roman Catholic theology, says Nygren, is based on a fusion of the two ideas (*op. cit., passim*). Augustine was the theological "father" who brought this to pass, along with his ideas of determinism, predestination, and original sin. His new idea of "love" he termed (in Latin) *caritas*, from which we have derived our word "charity," which has brought so much confusion in our King James Bibles as an attempt to translate *agape*. The medieval idea virtually eclipsed Gods grace.

For a brief time Luther tried to break up the synthesis to restore *agape* again. But after his death, his followers returned to the adulterated concept, because they could not relinquish the doctrine of the natural immortality of the soul. Practically all the churches, without any effective exception, have inherited this confused idea of love, along with Sunday observance, and the natural immortality of the soul from medieval Romanism. Some of their leaders must yearn almost pathetically to return to the pure New Testament truths, but do not as yet sense the way.

Wherever one finds the idea of the natural immortality of the soul, there he is sure to find self-centeredness as the dominant concept of love. It is as different from the New Testament idea of love as Sunday is different from Sabbath, yet is likewise a cleverly designed counterfeit. The doctrine of the natural immortality of the soul is a flag that warns us: here you will find no true understanding of the everlasting gospel of righteousness by faith because there can be no true idea of New Testament faith, certainly not that which is in harmony with the cleansing of the sanctuary.

This is one of the real reasons why Ellen White warned against the dangers of this false but subtle error. Ultimate Spiritualism is a false righteousness by faith:

> The popular ministry cannot successfully resist Spiritualism. They have nothing wherewith to shield their flocks from its baleful influence. ... The immortality of the soul ... is the foundation of Spiritualism. (1T 344).

> Through the two great errors, the immortality of the soul and Sunday sacredness. Satan will bring the people under his deceptions. While the former lays the foundation of Spiritualism, the latter creates a bond of sympathy with Rome ...

> As Spiritualism more closely imitates the nominal Christianity of the day, it has greater power to deceive and ensnare. Satan himself is converted, after the modern order of things. He will appear in the character of an angel of light. ... Protestants, having cast away the shield of truth, will also be deluded. Papists, Protestants and worldlings will alike accept the form of godliness without the power. (GC 588).

The simplicity of true godliness is buried beneath tradition.

The doctrine of the natural immortality of the soul is one error with which the enemy is deceiving man, this error is well-nigh universal ...

This is one of the lies forged in the synagogue of the enemy, one of the poisonous drafts of Babylon. (EV 247).

Why is it impossible for true New Testament love to exist in company with this "poisonous draft of Babylon"? Why can't Babylon see the cross, see *agape*, and experience genuine New Testament faith? Why can't she proclaim the true gospel?

Integral to the idea of the natural immortality of the soul is the view that Christ did not make an infinite sacrifice when He died on the cross. He tells the repentant thief, We'll get a great reward today. "*Today* shalt thou be with Me in paradise" (Luke 23:43). Yes, both supposedly went there that day! Throughout His ordeal, our Lord was sustained by the hope of reward and comforted by the assurance that He would not truly die. His sacrifice was only physical agony and human shame, of a temporary nature. Moses made an even greater sacrifice in behalf of Israel when he asked that his name be blotted from the Book of Life if Israel could not be forgiven (Ex. 32:32)! But in this popular view, the complete self-emptying nature of *agape* in Christ's love is neatly removed. He was motivated merely by egocentric concern; or at least the hope of reward was thoroughly mixed with His love.

But the true Biblical view is that Christ's sacrifice was truly infinite and eternal. Not only His human body "died"; He Himself died the equivalent of the "second death," the death without hope of resurrection. Himself being the infinite Son of God, such a sacrifice is the measure of infinite love, beyond our capacity to appreciate fully. Although He was indeed sustained by the bright assurance of His Father's favor up to the moment that darkness enveloped Calvary, there came over Him then the horror of a great darkness when He cried out, "My God, My God, why has Thou forsaken Me?" the Father's face was completely hidden. The full weight of our guilt was pressing upon Him. He then lost sight of the resurrection and a future reward:

> The Saviour could not see through the portals of the tomb. Hope did not present to Him His coming forth from the grave a conqueror, or tell Him of the Father's acceptance of the sacrifice. He feared that sin was so offensive to God that Their separation was to be eternal. Christ felt the anguish which the sinner will feel when mercy shall no longer plead for the guilty race. (DA 753).

It is this infinite dimension of Christ's love that is eclipsed by the pagan-papal doctrine of natural immortality. No church that holds to this concept can adequately appreciate the cross, or preach it in its proper power. This false doctrine further makes it impossible for the "*agape* of Christ" to constrain us truly, for its high fidelity realism is absent. And with *agape* thus adulterated, faith likewise is adulterated; and it is inevitable that righteousness be likewise shorn of its true dimensions. Nothing can come of it but disobedience to the law, continued sinning, self-centeredness, and lukewarmness, all cloaked as "salvation by faith."

Thus, when John says love (*agape*) is of God (1 John 4:7), he means that there can be no other source. "Herein is love (*agape*), not that we loved God, but that He loved us, and sent His Son to be the propitiation for our sins" (verse 10). But we can sum up live ways in which that "propitiation" is virtually denied or at least obscured, by this popular false doctrine. It creates a perplexity or hiatus: (1) The Father did not truly give His son but only *lent* Him; (2) His love was conditioned by a self-seeking anticipation of reward; (3) He made no real sacrifice beyond that which many martyrs have had to make, such as physical sufferings, but was sustained by more hope than many humans have when they die; (4) He did not truly die, but immediately entered a higher state of conscious existence in paradise; (5) at its very best, the love that "dwelt in the heart of Christ," so understood, was a synthesis of *agape* and *eros* identical to the *caritas* of Augustine, the basis of medieval Romanism.

Thus the cross is robbed of its true glory and New Testament love is nullified. Automatically therefore faith is likewise robbed of its true content, and is "dead," as James warns us. It cannot produce true obedience. Fear or concern for personal security remains the dominant motivation for the human soul. The cross cannot exercise its true power because it is enshrouded in mysterious confusion like a mountain peak encircled by clouds. No wonder Christ was concerned at the beginning of the process in the early church that led to the great apostasy — "thou hast left thy first agape." Until Evangelicalism sees and accepts the truth of the nature of man in the light of the cross, it will be quite unable to accept the cross of true Sabbath-keeping, or other "testing truths" of the third angel's message.

"The popular ministry" are ever so sincere, we know, and ever so earnest and devoted. But as a body they have no just appreciation of "the breadth, and length, and depth, and height" of the "*agape* of Christ, which passes knowledge" (Eph. 3:18, 19). Their false doctrines hide true love from them. Their concept of Christian love is much closer to the Catholic idea than to New Testament love. In its very highest forms, it cannot shed its egocentric motif. All this we can easily recognize.

Now, the crucial question is: *Do Seventh-day Adventists in general have the same basic idea of love as do the popular churches?* More specifically, do they have the same idea of "righteousness by faith" that the popular churches have in consequence of their belief in the natural immortality of the soul? According to the

True Witness of Revelation 3, "the angel of the church of the Laodiceans" has a problem in this respect, but honestly and sincerely "knows not" his true condition. Have the hands on the clock of time turned far enough for us to look at the past objectively?

If "the angel of the Church" were not "poor" in genuine New Testament faith and love, how could he repeatedly have borrowed "righteousness by faith" from these same popular churches who hold "the poisonous drafts of Babylon"? We can look at only a few revealing examples. The full story cannot yet be told:

(1) Because of a failure to appreciate the 1888 message, far back in the 1890's there was a tendency to confuse Quaker author Hannah Whitall Smith's *The Christian's Secret of a Happy Life* with true righteousness by faith, (cf. *General Conference Bulletin*, 1893, pp. 358, 359). Author Smith borrowed her ideas in turn from Fénelon, a Roman Catholic mystic at the court of Louis XIV, who spent his life energies trying to convert Protestants to Rome. (cf. *Great Controversy*, p. 272; *Britannica*, 1968, Vol. 9, p. 169). To this day Smith's (and therefore Fénelon's) ideas are endorsed by many as genuine righteousness by faith. This is the natural result of a sincere ignorance of the true contrast between Romanist and New Testament concepts of faith.

Through the decades there have been prominent examples of this confusion over Roman Catholic concepts of piety and the "interior life." It is considered popular and a mark of sophistication to be warmly appreciative of the teachings of Pascal and Fénelon. And indeed, there are scintillating gems of philosophical beauty in their works. The study of Fénelon's "self-renunciation" has been urged as virtually the same concept as taught in the writings of Ellen G. White, due to an unawareness of the import of *agape*. There seems to be a warmth of spiritual fervor that charms. It is not surprising that many youth have been innocently confused and misled.

This mixing of the true and the false is essentially the same process that led to Augustine's mixture of *agape* and Hellenistic love which was the foundation of medieval Romanism. The lack of discernment was and is the problem. How could such confusion have existed had there been a clear understanding of the message the Lord gave this people in 1888? It is fallacy to assume that false concepts are purified when mixed with Spirit of Prophecy quotations as though arsenic could be nullified if mixed with flour.

In the same era of the 1890's, there was a tendency to confuse Rome's concepts of "righteousness by faith" with the 1888 message. This was also due to a failure to appreciate the message the Lord sent us. Thus the uncertainty regarding the 1888 message prepared the stage for a succession of Seventh-day Adventist pilgrimages to non-Adventist theologians to find help in understanding and proclaiming "righteousness by faith."

> Some of the brethren, since the Minneapolis meeting, I have heard myself say "amen" to preaching, to statements that were utterly heathen, and did not know but that it was the righteousness of Christ. Some of those who stood so openly against that at that time, and voted with uplifted hand against it, ... since that time I have heard say "amen" to statements that were as openly and decidedly papal as the papal church itself can state them. (*General Conference Bulletin*, 1893, p. 244; A.T. Jones).

> That you may have the two things — the truth of justification by faith, and the falsity of it — side by side, I will read what this [Catholic belief] says, and then what God says in *Steps to Christ* ... I want you to see what the Roman Catholic idea of justification by faith is, because I have had to meet it among

professed Seventh-day Adventists the past four years right straight through. These very things, these very expressions that are in this Catholic book as to what justification by faith is and how to obtain it, are just such expressions as professed Seventh-day Adventists have made to me as to what justification by faith is.

I want to know how you and I can carry a message to this world, warning them against the worship of the beast when we hold in our very profession the doctrines of the beast. ... It is high time that Seventh-day Adventists understood it (*Ibid.*, p. 261, 262. See also pages 265, 266).

Many today sincerely believe that the Lord honored the Sunday-keeping churches who hold to the natural immortality of the soul by vouchsafing to them the "same light" of righteousness by faith that He gave to us in 1888. According to this view, those who hold these "two great errors," these "poisonous drafts of Babylon," understand and are heralding to the world the true "everlasting gospel." This confused conviction actually strikes at the very heart of Seventh-day Adventist existence by questioning the uniqueness of "the everlasting gospel" as the Lord entrusted true concepts of righteousness by faith to us:

Others, not of our faith, were being moved to restudy *the same truth* of Righteousness by Faith, at about the same time [1888], which is historically true, as noted elsewhere. (*Movement of Destiny*, p. 255, footnote, emphasis added.)

We have not been too well aware of these paralleling spiritual movements — of organizations outside the Advent Movement — having the same general burden and emphasis, and arising at about the same time. ... *The impulse manifestly came from the same Source.* And in timing, Righteousness by Faith centered in the year 1888.

For example, the renowned Keswick Conferences ... the Northfield Bible Conferences, founded by Dwight L. Moody,

... men like Murray, Simpson, Gordon, Holden, Meyer, McNeil, Moody, Waugh, McConkey, Scroggie, Howden, Smith, McKensie, McIntosh, Brooks, Dixon, Kyle, Morgan, Needham, [A.T.] Pierson, Seiss, Thomas, West and a score of others — all giving this [1888] general emphasis. Untold numbers have known and been blessed by their writings. And this includes *many of our own men*. (*Ibid.*, pp. 319-321, emphasis added).

It is only fair that we recognize that the author saw there were limitations in these non-Adventists' concepts. But this only more sharply points up the real problem: Many through these long decades have not recognized that there are two entirely separate and antithetical "schools" of righteousness by faith, one having its source in Christ and His apostles, and the other having its source in the great "falling away" that is coming to its successive final stages in the "fall of Babylon" since 1844. These two "schools" hold antithetical views of New Testament love and faith. Instead, we have supposed that "the popular ministry" automatically understand the true gospel — they just don't go "far enough."

(2) In the 1920's and 1930's the record shows that many of us wholeheartedly and enthusiastically accepted and endorsed the *Sunday School Times* ideas of righteousness by faith known as "The Victorious Life." This history illustrates the truth of our Lord's words that we desperately need to "buy" of *Him* "gold," and not from "the popular ministry":

(a) The first step seemed to be the publication of *The Doctrine of Christ* (*Review and Herald*, 1919). The author quotes from some unknown source, approvingly, in support of "The Victorious Life" idea. Investigation reveals that the author's source was a book written by Robert C. McQuilkin, Corresponding Secretary, Victorious Life Conferences, Princeton and Cedar Lake, 1918, published by Headquarters for Victorious Life Literature, Philadelphia. The editor of the *Sunday School Times* wrote the foreword of McQuilkin's book:

> It was the new and undiscovered country of the Victorious Life that brought us together, Bob McQuilkin and me, ... the foreign land of undreamed riches and delights. ... I am glad that he is now sharing his findings and his convictions with many, through these studies in the Victorious Life. (Charles G. Trumbull, *Victorious Life Studies*, Foreword).

(b) *The Doctrine of Christ* forthwith began its work among us and soon we find able, prominent speakers one by one supporting the imported concepts. "The Victorious Life" solidly established the egocentric, "Evangelical" concept of love in the Seventh-day Adventist Church and led the church thoroughly away from the concepts of righteousness by faith that made the 1888 message unique. As with Fénelon, the program was to search for Ellen G. White quotations that appeared, out of context, to support the Sunday School Times ideas, quotations which really cannot be understood except in the context in which she wrote them — the 1888 message. A theological thesis in the Seminary says of this history:

> About the same time [1920] ... various denominational leaders were giving thought to what was termed the "victorious life." ... At the General Conference session of 1922. ... A.G. Daniells in addressing the delegates, stated that he had come to believe in what was being termed the "victorious life" ...

> O. Montgomery, at the time vice-president of the South American Division, and later one of the general vice-presidents of the world organization, stated that "much emphasis" had been given to that theme "of late." He referred to articles written for denominational journals and sermons that he had heard. He was under the impression that some considered it a phase of Christian experience unknown

before. He showed that it was the very same experience that Adventists had spoken of as a part of justification and righteousness by faith ...

C.H. Watson, at the time one of the vice-presidents of the General Conference, capitalized the "victorious life" idea in a Week of Prayer Reading for 1923. (*Developments in the Teaching of Justification and Righteousness by Faith in the Seventh-day Adventist Church after 1900*, by Bruno William Steinweg, 1948, pp. 39-43).

Bear in mind that these speakers of the 1920's were the same brethren whom Dr. Froom quotes as insisting that the 1888 message was accepted. (*Op. cit.*, pp. 681- 686).

(c) The religious revival that swept the popular churches in that era was adopted by our brethren, enthusiastically. We do not find in the files of the *Review* dissenting voices of any who discerned that "The Victorious Life" was a fulfillment of the following warning in *Great Controversy:*

Before the time for such a movement shall come [the Loud Cry], he [Satan] will endeavor to prevent it by introducing a *counterfeit*. ... He will make it appear that God's special blessing is poured out; there will be manifest what is thought to be great religious interest. Multitudes will exult that God is working marvelously for them, when the work is that of *another spirit*. (GC 464, emphasis added.)

Following is a sampling of the pronouncements of writers in the *Review and Herald:*

"The Victorious Life" is only another expression for "righteousness by faith." (R&H, Nov. 11, 1920).

"The Victorious Life" is nothing more nor less than simple Bible Christianity. (Editor, R&H, July 6, 1922).

The following excerpts are taken verbatim from a little book on righteousness by faith of that era which illustrate the constant leaning on what Ellen White spoke of as "the popular ministry":

> Cortland Myers says, Dr. L. Munhall said, says Cortland Myers, Robert F. Horton says, Henry Van Dyke says, wrote ... Whitefield Edwards says, Dr. W.T. Grenfell says, at the feet of D.L. Moody. Charles Dickens said, Sherwood Eddy said, Bishop Hannington said, Amos R. Wells has said. Charles G. Finney once said, D.L. Moody says, Forrest Hallenbeck says, John Wesley ... said, John R. Mott says, Charles G. Trumbull says, *Sunday School Times* says ...
>
> (*Alone With God*, Pacific Press).

A ready example of the confusion that has prevailed was the attempt to make Ellen G. White endorse "The Victorious Life" enthusiasm by entitling one of her letters accordingly (see *Testimonies to Ministers*, pp. 516-520). This is understandable as the book was compiled during the height of the movement (1922).

(3) We must look at the 1926 General Conference Session that was held in Milwaukee. It was a great occasion and the delegates who gathered there were deeply in earnest. They never dreamed that the work would still be unfinished over half a century later:

> It is the hope and belief of all that this session of the Conference will be marked as an unusually spiritual one. A conviction seems to have taken possession of many that the time has fully come for this movement to go forward in a mighty movement for the finishing of the work. (Carlyle B. Haynes, *General Conference Bulletin*, 1926, p. 3).

An earnest and sincere writer tells us that the 1926 Conference is more important than the 1888 one:

> It is my firm opinion that it would be well to give less emphasis to 1888 and more emphasis to 1926. In fact, the

General Conference of 1926 was what 1888 might have been, had there been greater unanimity on the meaning of the gospel. (Norval F. Pease, *The Faith That Saves*, p. 59).

In searching for evidence that we have truly accepted the Lord's message of righteousness by faith, some cite the 1926 General Conference Session as an example of positive "victory." The messages given were deeply spiritual and fervent. It was one of our finest Sessions, no doubt.

One author suggests: "No more positive evidence of spiritual growth and maturity [since 1888] could be presented than the sermons of 1926" (Pease, *op. cit.*). In other words, the strongest evidence for the acceptance of the 1888 message is the 1926 Session messages.

But as one examines those messages, what does he find? An almost complete absence of the basic motifs that made the 1888 message unique! Without realizing it, our brethren in 1926 had gotten away from the message that was intended to finish Gods work and had been deeply influenced by the "Victorious Life" borrowing from "the popular ministry." Let us say that they were wonderful, godly, dedicated, marvelous men and women. We like to think of our forebears that way. *But did they possess the "gold"?* Two facts make the answer clear: (a) If the 1888 message began to supply the need, as Ellen White said; the 1926 messages lack that content. This can be proven by motif analysis. (b) The passage of over half a century since 1926 makes suspect the claim that the 1926 Conference was a victory where 1888 was a defeat.

Shortly afterwards, Elder A.G. Daniells published his celebrated and valuable *Christ Our Righteousness*. It contains very frank statements admitting that the 1888 message was never truly accepted (pp. 39, 55, 58, 59, 63, 79, 86, 1926 ed.). But the author did not accurately reproduce the 1888 message itself.

Practically none of the unique aspects of the 1888 message find expression there. Even the Ellen G. White quotations used seem selected in such a way as to avoid them or filter them out.

In the conclusion of his book seeking to summarize his idea of "entering through the door of faith," he falls back onto an emphasis on man's own efforts (pp. 130, 131). He betrays reliance on the key thought of legalism some seven times in one paragraph alone — "we should" do this or that (pp. 131, 132). Such exhortations — "we should" pray more, "we should" believe more, "we should" read our Bibles more, "we should" be more earnest, "we should" sacrifice more — appear frequently in the earnest appeals of our general leaders of those days. They demonstrate an ignorance of true New Testament motivation — genuine faith which automatically produces full consecration.

Daniells concludes his book with a one-sided emphasis on justification to the exclusion of true sanctification, a concept much closer to the *Sunday School Times'* "victorious life" idea than to the 1888 concept of getting ready for translation:

> And every day that comes and goes we should humbly plead before the throne of grace the merits, the perfect obedience, of Christ in the place of our transgressions and sins. And in doing this, we should believe and realize that our justification comes through Christ as our substitute and surety, that He has died for us, and He is our atonement and righteousness … (*Christ Our Righteousness*, p. 132).

In fact, not once in his book does Elder Daniells seem able to recognize that Christ is our example as well as "substitute." The author was earnest and sincere and his book is indeed valuable; but it clearly shows the influence of the "victorious life" enthusiasm in drawing us away from the real heart of the 1888 message. (For example, see Daniells' summary of "the gospel" on pages 117, 118, 1926 ed.).

We can agree with one author when he says that Elder Daniells' stand in this book "was in perfect harmony with the best evangelical teaching" (*By Faith Alone*, p. 189) But "perfect harmony" with the finest orthodox evangelical teaching of the past and of Daniells' contemporaries in "the popular ministry" is not good enough to hasten the coming of the Lord. The past half a century can demonstrate that clearly. In fact, the confusion of present-day "Reformationist" justification by faith can be traced to the popular emphases among us of the 1920's. This constant leaning on non-Adventist theologians and universities and popular Evangelical leaders retards rather than advances the Seventh-day Adventist cause.

Elder Daniells significantly analyzes an Ellen G. White prediction that "false theories and erroneous ideas will take minds captive, Christ and His righteousness will be dropped out of the experience of many, and their faith will be without power or life," unless the 1888 message is truly accepted (R&H, Sept. 3, 1889). He says:

> To a lamentable degree, God's people *failed* to bring the divine power into their experience, and the result predicted *has been seen:*
>
> 1. False theories and erroneous ideas *have* taken minds captive.
> 2. Christ and His righteousness *have* been dropped out of the experience of many. (*Op. cit.*, p. 108, emphasis added).

Our history had demonstrated the truth of Elder Daniells' analysis far more graphically than he could ever have imagined.

(4) In the 1950's we borrowed and endorsed the Methodist missionary E. Stanley Jones' concepts of "righteousness by faith" and recommended them to our ministers as "safe." Jones' concepts "would enrich one's ministry," said *The Ministry*

(February, 1950). Yet Jones' preoccupation with the idea of the natural immortality of the soul causes him to confuse telepathic communication with the dead with the reception of the Holy Spirit, and also to confess that "Christ Himself has deficiencies which are to be supplied by other faiths" (*The Message of Sat Tul Ashram*, pp. 285, 291). It was Jones who coined the slogan, "Share Your Faith," which we eagerly adopted; but Jones meant that "this sharing means not only giving out what one has to non-Christians, but the sharing of what they have in their own faiths ... Christ Himself has deficiencies" (*Ibid.*). What a source for our "righteousness by faith"!

We find one lone, dissenting public voice in the church paper at last protesting this borrowing from E. Stanley Jones. Elder W.A. Spicer wrote an article for the *Review* which was published during the summer of 1950, exposing the falseness of his ideas, mentioning Jones by name. (In the spring of 1950 he had published an article containing an oblique warning).

(5) The 1952 Bible Conference (September 1-13 in the Sligo Church) claimed to recover the 1888 message and even to go beyond it. One prominent speaker said:

> To a large degree the church failed to build on the foundation laid at the 1888 General Conference. Much has been lost as a result. We are years behind. ... Long ere this we should have been in the Promised Land.

> But the message of righteousness by faith given in the 1888 Conference has been repeated here. Practically every speaker from the first day onward has laid great stress upon this all-important doctrine, and there was no prearranged plan that he should do so. ... Truly this one subject has, in this conference "swallowed up every other."

> And this great truth has been given here in this 1952 Bible Conference with far greater power than it was given in the 1888 Conference because those who have spoken here have

had the advantage of much added light shining forth from hundreds of pronouncements on this subject in the writings of the Spirit of Prophecy which those who spoke back there did not have.

The light of justification and righteousness by faith shines upon us today more clearly than it ever shone before upon any people.

No longer will the question be, "What was the attitude of our workers and people toward the message of righteousness by faith that was given in 1888? What did they do bout it?" From now on the great question must be, "What did we do with the light on righteousness by faith as proclaimed in the 1952 Bible Conference?" (W.H. Branson, *Our Firm Foundation*, vol. 2. pp. 616, 617).

Since then over three decades have passed by — time enough to finish God's work There was no official opposition to the 1952 message. "Practically every speaker" proclaimed it, and apparently everyone accepted it. And the speakers were the "angel of the church of the Laodiceans" — the church leadership. If the 1952 message was a true recovery of the 1888 message, the work should have been finished shortly afterward, for it was given "with far greater power" than in 1888. The 1952 brethren were "richer" than "any people" in world history! They had the "gold."

But a careful study of the 1952 messages fails to disclose the basic motifs that made the 1888 message unique. Like the 1926 messages on righteousness by faith, they present no light beyond what the church has been preaching for many decades. Somehow the truths that Ellen White endorsed in 1888 eluded our brethren of 1952. This is understandable, for with the possible exceptions of one or two they had very likely never actually studied the 1888 message in its original context. (Even today few have).

Elder Branson claimed that in spite of its lukewarmness the church had a "perfect system of truth." He failed to see that "the gospel of Christ ... is the power of God unto salvation," and that if the church truly possessed the "gospel of Christ" in its fulness, the "power" would be automatic. Thus he failed to recognize the basic principle of "righteousness by faith' — that if one has the faith, the righteousness is sure to be there too. He claimed we are rich in the very thing the True Witness says we are poor in. He expressed no need on the part of the speakers to understand true righteousness by faith, but claimed for them an "impulse by the Spirit of God" "far greater" than Ellen White claimed for the messengers sent in 1888.

Careful motif analysis can demonstrate that the messages of the 1926 and 1952 meetings prepared the way for the current confusion of so-called "Reformationist" concepts of justification by faith in place of the unique truths divinely entrusted to Seventh-day Adventists.

If one will read through both volumes of *Our Firm Foundation*, where "practically every speaker ... laid great stress upon this all-important doctrine [righteousness by faith]," he will find an astounding fact emerge. Not one speaker recognized the danger that the Lords servant warned of in the passage quoted above (GC 464) nor did one discern that the popular churches' interpretation of righteousness by faith is devoid of New Testament love. No one discerned a relation between the ministry of the heavenly High Priest in the Most Holy Apartment and an understanding of true righteousness by faith. It is amazing that the following quotation from *Early Writings* was not referred to once:

> Those who rose up with Jesus would send up their faith to Him in the holiest [the Most Holy Apartment], and pray, "My Father, give us Thy Spirit." Then Jesus would breathe

upon them the Holy Ghost. In that breath was light power, and much *love*, joy and peace.

I turned to look at the company who were still bowed before the throne [who had not followed Christ by faith into the Most Holy Apartment]; they did not know that Jesus had left it. Satan appeared to be by the throne, trying to carry on the work of God. I saw them look up to the throne, and pray, "Father, give us Thy Spirit." Satan would then breathe upon them an unholy influence: in it there was light and much power, but no sweet love, joy and peace. (EW 55, 56).

The setting of this passage is critically important, for it has a direct bearing on our understanding of the gospel itself "The company who were still bowed before the throne" is the group who rejected the sanctuary truth in the 1844 era. Although the imagery is highly symbolic, it is clear Ellen White was referring to the change in Christ's ministry at the end of the 2300 years. Those who did not appreciate the change exposed themselves to a lethal deception — Satan masquerading as the "Christ" in a ministry which the true High Priest had now "left."

But this tragic deception is not limited to people living in that immediate post-1844 era. Churches which embrace the doctrine of natural immortality are *exposed to the same frightful danger*. In this time when the sanctuary doctrine is being boldly challenged by many within the Seventh-day Adventist church, we need to see that a rejection of this unique Seventh-day Adventist sanctuary doctrine entails also a rejection of the pure New Testament gospel of righteousness by faith:

Many who professed to love Jesus, and who shed tears as they read the story of the cross, derided the good news of His (second) coming. ... Those who rejected the first angel's message could not be benefitted by the second; neither were they benefitted by the midnight cry, which was to prepare them to enter with Jesus by faith into the most holy place of the heavenly sanctuary. And by rejecting the two former messages, they have so darkened their understanding that they can see no light in the third angel's message, which shows the way into the most holy place. I saw that as the Jews crucified Jesus, so the nominal churches had crucified these messages, and therefore they have (note present tense) no knowledge of the way into the most holy, and they can not be benefitted by the intercession of Jesus there. Like the Jews, who offered their useless sacrifices, they offer up their useless prayers to the apartment which Jesus has left; Satan, pleased with the deception, assumes a religious character, and leads the minds of these professed Christians to himself, working with his power, his signs and lying wonders, to fasten them in his snare.. He also comes as an angel of light and spreads his influence over the land by means of false reformations. The churches are elated, and consider that God is working marvelously for them, when it is the work of another spirit. (EW 55, 56).

In many of the revivals which have occurred during the last half century, the same influences have been at work to a greater or less degree ... an emotional excitement, a mingling of the true with the false, that is well adapted to deceive. (CC 464).

No awareness of the danger of this counterfeit gospel of the orthodox "popular ministry" found expression throughout the 1952 Bible Conference.

(6) In the 1960's we eagerly adopted ideas and methods from Campus Crusade for Christ, sending ministers to their headquarters to learn from them how to present "righteousness by faith." This can be attested by the wide prominence given to their *Four Spiritual Laws* and similar substitutes that we prepared ourselves from time to time. Some of our men worked with the Campus Crusade group very closely, but this enthusiasm seemed to be cooled by Campus Crusade's reported insistence

that all their workers subscribe to the doctrine of the natural immortality of the soul. This is essential to their concepts of righteousness by faith.

Campus Crusade's *Four Spiritual Laws* are thoroughly egocentric. The "righteousness by faith" they present is not parallel to or consistent with the work that Christ is doing in the Most Holy Apartment Those who have used them and supposed they accomplished much good with them have not realized that this brand of "righteousness by faith" is as far from true New Testament teaching as Sunday is from Sabbath-keeping.

(7) In the recent decade (the 1970's) we have eagerly turned to the message and methods of the famed "church growth" experts and proponents, hoping to find there principles of "evangelism explosion" that will work with us as they do with them. As in all the previous movements for decades, the concept of love (and consequently the concept of faith) is thoroughly egocentric. Yet we seek to validate these concepts by searching for Spirit of Prophecy support for them. The implication is very clear: God has given to the popular ministry the "gold tried in the fire," and we are to go "buy" of them. He has entrusted to them the secret of finishing the work The confusion goes back to the post-1888 history.

Thus, like Israel of old, we have wandered in a kind of spiritual wilderness for many decades, not understanding the message the Lord sent to us.

Through "our" failure to receive the 1888 message for what it truly was, we have been reading the Spirit of Prophecy with a "veil" over our eyes, the same one that the Jews had (cf. 2 Cor. 3:15). It is the same "veil" that hung over the eyes of the brethren who attended the 1888 Conference to whom the Lords servant said, "I have been talking and pleading with you, but it does not seem to make any difference with you" (MS. 9, 1888). They had the living presence of the prophet with them, and it made no

95

difference with them. We have her books with us. But they too have made no difference because we have unwittingly accepted the "popular ministry's" ideas of righteousness by faith in place of the true. In fact, we quite officially see no distinction between their doctrine in that respect and that which God has for us. (cf. *Movement of Destiny*, pp. 255-258, 319-321, 616-628).

So much have we failed to realize and appreciate the uniqueness of our message of righteousness by faith that we have moved from our positions on "the remnant church" and the proclamation of the "everlasting gospel" as being emphatically and clearly unique. Now we say that some popular evangelical churches and organizations who keep Sunday and hold to the natural immortality of the soul, those "poisonous drafts of Babylon" (Ev. 247) are a part of the true remnant church and are proclaiming the everlasting gospel to the world. The implication is clear that the "everlasting gospel" of the three angels' messages has been entrusted by heaven to "many of the evangelical churches" whose "whole new missionary zeal" has significantly postponed the fall of Babylon beginning in the early 19th century (cf. *Mission Possible*, by Gottfried Oosterwal, pp. 32-39). We need to ask a very serious question: Is this "whole new missionary zeal" indeed a genuine proclamation of "the everlasting gospel" "in verity"? Or are we being blinded by "an angel of light" and his "false reformations"?

How can those who hold to the "poisonous drafts of Babylon," the natural immortality of the soul and Sunday sacredness and who do not understand the Atonement clearly give the "everlasting gospel" to the world? True, the great mass of Gods people are in the popular churches, and they are sincere. We must respect them and truly "cooperate" with them in every good work. But is our "mission" virtually a me-too voice proclaiming what is basically the same gospel? Is there no clearly unique message to call Gods people "Out"?

Nothing is said here to be critical or disrespectful toward the brethren of the past ninety years and those living today who have sincerely assumed that "the popular ministry" understand the "same truth of righteousness by faith' the Lord gave us in 1888. Nothing is said here with a fault-finding spirit We are simply looking at the Laodicean message and inquiring how it can be true that we do indeed need to buy *of our Lord* "gold tried in the fire."

The 1888 message constituted a genuine revival of the original New Testament idea of *agape* and its complementary response, faith. Thus, its concept of justification by faith was unique and distinct from that of the "popular ministry." Freed at last from the confusion of the egocentric idea of the natural immortality of the soul, the 1888 message was able to restate the apostolic ideas more clearly. With the sole exception of Luther, who only partially reached this goal, one searches almost in vain through history to find another similar breakthrough. Most of the 16th to 18th century Reformers were still shackled to the pagan-papal idea which had its origin in Hellenism, Calvin and Wesley for example. They searched for the breakthrough but could never truly find it.

Is it not time that this confusion concerning love and faith be resolved in the remnant church? There is such a thing as the Seventh-day Adventist conscience. Does that conscience recognize the need that our True Witness says is ours?

If what we have understood and preached since 1926 or longer is the "same truth" as that "beginning" of the Latter Rain and the Loud Cry of 1888, will someone please tell us why the work has not yet been finished, nor the earth been lightened with the glory of the fourth angel?

8

The Divinely Appointed Remedies: "White Raiment" and "Eyesalve"

The "white raiment, that thou mayest be clothed" is said to be a "spotless character made pure in the blood of their dear Redeemer" (3T 254), "the righteousness of Christ" (5T 233), or "the robe of Christ's righteousness" (ML 311). Ellen White made frequent applications of it to the 1888 "message of Christ's righteousness." John himself says it is "the righteousness of saints" (Rev. 19:8), obviously not their own for they have none, but Christ's at last fully imparted to them, not merely imputed in a strictly and exclusively legal sense.

Had there been no "presentation of the righteousness of Christ in the relation to the law as the doctor [Waggoner] has placed it before us [in 1888] (cf. Ms. 15, 1888) the Seventh-day Adventist ministry and church would have been embarrassingly "naked". We had preached the law until we were as "dry as the hills of Gilboa." On the stage in view of the universe of God, we were assuming that we were proclaiming the "everlasting gospel" to the world when we did not even understand "the third angel's message in verity." The 1888 message was to invest "the Advent message" with precious content and the church with precious experience that would truly remove cause for "shame."

Was our nakedness clothed at that time? Or are we still naked? Is "Christ's righteousness" now a meaningful concept to us? Is it a cliché, words that mask a void? Has His "wife ... made herself ready"? Does she know Christ so well that she is at last fitted to be His mate? If not, then she is not yet "clothed."

Is her knowledge of His righteousness as superficial as that of the "seven women" who take hold of Him and seek to be called by His name, who can never become His true Bride (cf. Isa. 4:1-4)? Christ was not a mere shibboleth to the 1888 messengers. They did not mouth His name and sprinkle their messages with histrionic, emotional presentations calculated to impress. They had a distinct, objective view of Christ that was communicable in terms of doctrinal truth. They saw something that apparently none of their contemporary brethren had ever seen. This is clearly evident from what Ellen White said:

> I see the beauty of truth in the presentation of the righteousness of Christ in relation to the law as the doctor [Waggoner] has placed it before us. You say, many of you, it is light and truth. Yet you have not presented it in this light heretofore. ... If our ministering brethren would accept the doctrine which has been presented so clearly -the righteousness of Christ in connection with the law — and I know they need to accept this, their prejudices would not have a controlling power, and the people would be fed with their portion of meat in due season. (MS 15. 1888, Olson, *Through Crisis to Victory*, p. 295).

When Brother Waggoner brought out these ideas at Minneapolis, it was the first clear teaching on this subject from any human lips I had heard, excepting the conversations between myself and my husband. (MS 5, 1889).

The unique message these brethren brought at that time was given a special name — "the doctrine ... of the righteousness of Christ in connection with the law." It was a recognition that Christ's righteousness was that of a true divine human being who "condemned sin in the flesh," having been sent "in the likeness of sinful flesh" (Rom. 8:3). This was the focal point of their message, its dominant theme that gave it a practical keynote. Without this "big idea" their message would have been powerless. The character Christ developed we can develop, if we only have His faith. In other words, righteousness is by faith!

Both messengers specifically denied that Christ came in the nature of Adam before the fall. (cf. Waggoner, *Christ and His Righteousness*, pp. 26-30; Jones, *The Consecrated Way*, pp. 21-44 together with the *General Conference Bulletin*, 1895, pp. 232-234, 265-270). They specifically stated that He "took" the nature of man after the Fall, and in the most explicit, emphatic way affirmed a view of Christ entirely different from that which is ordinarily and widely proclaimed today. (There are of course some exceptions here and there, and in very recent years some publications have begun to present the 1888 view of Christ's righteousness). If our current popular view of "Christ's righteousness" is true, then the basic heart of Jones' and Waggoner's message was positively wrong, and Ellen White was wrong to endorse it as she did.

Earnest efforts are made to gather statements from Ellen White that seem to affirm that she opposed the view of Jones and Waggoner. These are pitted against numerous statements that support Jones' and Waggoner's view. The net result is confusion. It appears to this day that no theologian has arisen who is able to reconcile the apparently contradictory nature of these two sets of statements. Wherever the subject is discussed, one set of statements is invariably used to cancel out the other. But Ellen White would be a false messenger if she so contradicted herself!

None of us will be able to understand these apparently irreconcilable statements until we study them in their true context, the 1888 message brought by Jones and Waggoner. "Letters have been coming to me, affirming that Christ could not have had the same nature as man, for if He had, He would have fallen under similar temptations." (Morning Talk Jan. 29, 1890, R&H, Feb. 18, 1890; 1SM 408). It is very obvious that these letters were criticisms from the field regarding

Jones' and Waggoner's presentation of the "message of Christ's righteousness." How can we understand her comments on the letters unless we understand the controverted message? Though the letters are probably unavailable, we still have access in the archives to the important thing — what Ellen White endorsed as the "beginning" of the Latter Rain and the Loud Cry.

It can be questioned if this generation has seen such powerful presentations of "Christ's righteousness in relation to the law" as in the 1895 *Bulletin* and in Jones' *The Consecrated Way*. Never has the Book of Psalms been so revealed as the most Christ-centered book of the Bible as it is in those studies. Had it not been for the non-committal attitude and opposition of a great proportion of our brethren in the 1890's, "the revelation of Christ's righteousness" in these messages would have wrought a miracle in those days, and the church would have been clothed with "white raiment" as she went forth to proclaim the Loud Cry to the world. Christ would have been vindicated in His people as they demonstrated in their sinful flesh the faithful reflection of what He demonstrated in "the likeness of sinful flesh" when He was on earth. Having seen Jesus clearly revealed, they would have received "the faith of Jesus." Christ and His righteousness have not yet been clearly seen.

Another view has replaced the 1888 message of Christ's righteousness: Christ had to take the sinless nature of Adam before the Fall, and therefore it is not possible for His perfect character to be manifested in our sinful flesh. This view is virtually identical to that held by those who observe Sunday and hold to the natural immortality of the soul. None of the "popular ministry" has any clear concept of "Christ's righteousness," although a sincere effort to grasp it may be detected in such writers as Reinhold Niebuhr, C.S. Lewis, and some others. But no church or movement holds to the unique view that God gave to Seventh-day Adventists in 1888. We still have the field clear!

"What difference does it make?" is the question many ask. Only a legalistic frame of mind could ask such a question. The concept of "Christ's righteousness" is meaningless to those motivated by an egocentric concern, except as a legalistic, judicial maneuver to cover up our continued unrighteousness. The emphasis on legally "imputed righteousness" has become so heavy that for the average Christian there remains no foreseeable possibility that he can ever become truly like Christ in character.

Such concepts make an actual preparation for Christ's coming and translation seem to be an experience so visionary and remote as to belong in the next century or beyond.

The following quotation is often pressed into service to support the heavy emphasis on legally imputed righteousness. The first sentence is emphasized and the context slighted. Note carefully that this statement is not an oblique rebuke of the 1888 messengers — Ellen White firmly supported their message at this time. She is referring to the "popular ministry's" counterfeit teaching on "righteousness by faith," and her true emphasis on imparted righteousness:

> When it is in the heart to obey God, when efforts are put forth to this end, Jesus accepts this disposition and effort as man's best service, and He makes up for the deficiency with His own divine merit But He will not accept those who claim to have faith in Him, and yet are disloyal to His father's commandment. We hear a great deal about faith, but we need to hear a great deal more about works. Many are deceiving their own souls by living an easy-going, accommodating, crossless religion. But Jesus says, "If any man will come after Me, let him deny himself, and take up his cross and follow Me." (ST, June 16, 1890; 1SM 382).

But this is commonly interpreted to mean, "if you say you love the Lord, 'it is in the heart to obey God', so just try a little to be good. You can't obey the commandments, and the Lord knows it, so He'll be satisfied and 'make up' for it all 'with His own divine merit'."

Take the problems of sex, for example. While promiscuity, infidelity, and divorce make frightening inroads into the church, most of our well-intentioned ministers continue to hold to a view that Christ took the sinless nature of Adam before the Fall, and by implication therefore He could not possibly have been tempted to fornication or adultery. Adam certainly was not so tempted! The official view taught in *Questions on Doctrine* is that Christ "was exempt from the inherited passions and pollutions that corrupt the natural descendants of Adam" (p. 383). This is a rather confused statement, for it implies a contradiction of both the Bible and the Spirit of Prophecy. The authors could have made it only because of ignorance or disregard of the 1888 concept of Christ's righteousness.

Christ was not "exempt" from anything. Heaven forbid! The only reason He did not sin was that he chose not to sin, not because of any advantaged "exemption" that made temptation less tempting to Him than to us. He *chose* not to sin because He knew how to die to self and demonstrated it by dying on His cross. Thus he "condemned sin in the flesh" (Rom. 8:3) including sexual sin, which He was as much tempted to "in the flesh" as anybody else. He was "in *all* points tempted like as we are, yet without sin" (Heb. 4:15). If we deny this, there is no message of Christ's righteousness, for Christ's righteousness would be meaningless apart from the context of inheriting the "likeness of sinful flesh" that any son or daughter of Adam receives.

But many don't understand this. Ignorance of this truth severs their bond of union and sympathy with Christ. This is why thousands have nothing to hold them in their hours of temptation and Christ is openly humiliated by a remnant church that offers no appreciably higher moral excellence than do the churches that hold to those "poisonous drafts of Babylon."

One needs only to wrestle with the problems found in mission fields or of a modern city church to realize that we are desperately "naked' in this area of "righteousness," Our True Witness says, "I counsel thee to buy of *Me* … white raiment, that thou mayest be clothed, and that the shame of thy nakedness do not appear" (Rev. 3: 18). We are not counseled to "buy" it of "the popular ministry," but of *Him*. How can we "buy" of Him? The following gives a clue:

> The Lord in His great mercy sent a most precious message to His people through Elders Waggoner and Jones. This message was to bring more prominently before the world the uplifted Saviour, the sacrifice for the sins of the whole world. … It invited the people to receive the righteousness of Christ, which is made manifest in obedience to all the commandments of God. Many had lost sight of Jesus. … This is the message that God commanded to be given to the world. (TM 91, 92).

Note the source of the message: "The *Lord* … sent." How better could we "buy" of Him except to surrender our false concepts and humbly accept the "message of Christ's righteousness" that he sent to this people, but which is not understood today?

It is "the angel of the church" who is so counseled. It is not enough for us to stand idly by maintaining a neutral stance in a time of crisis. We are to "buy" of Him — actually receive. The message should be widely proclaimed by every means available, in our books, our periodicals, our youth magazines, proclaimed over the radio and TV, and taught in our institutions of learning, as well as Sabbath by Sabbath in our pulpits. The mere issuance of a few booklets containing the message will not suffice. In the 1888 decade, the messengers were permitted the opportunity of proclaiming the message themselves in various ways available to them. But the movement failed because the ministry as a whole did not wholeheartedly throw themselves into the glorious proclamation of the message. Aside from Ellen White, the very best support the messengers were given was half-hearted. (One prominent historian recognizes that when the dark decade of the 1890's turned into the 20th century, no effective messenger among us other than Ellen White was proclaiming the message. (cf. Norval Pease, *By Faith Alone*, p. 164).

Certainly a neutral stance today would be an improvement over outright opposition. But that would not answer the call of the True Witness. Neutrality will never ensure the finishing of Gods work in this generation. We must do better than the Persian government in the days of Queen Esther who stood neutrally and merely permitted the Jews to defend themselves. We have no illusions regarding our previous attitudes being infallible as the Medes and Persians considered their decrees that could never be altered. The time has come now to support the truth wholeheartedly.

Let the "tidings of Christ's righteousness" permeate the church worldwide. Let the truth go to work And let our modern methods of communication be fully employed in proclaiming what Ellen White said is "a most precious message" which "the Lord in His great mercy sent," "just what the people needed."

Only then could it honestly be said that we did our best to obey our Lord so that we could confidently expect He would answer our prayers for revival and reformation in preparation for the Latter Rain and the Loud Cry.

Our Lord utters another sentence when He proposes a third remedy: "And anoint thine eyes with eyesalve, that thou mayest see." (Rev. 3: 18).

The eyesalve is to enable us to:
"Detect sin under any guise" (4T88).
"Discern necessities of the time" (CT 42).

"Distinguish between truth and error" (ML 73).

"See and shun Satan's wiles" (5T 233).

In this context our blindness is seen to be another term for being spiritually unconscious. The "eyesalve" is that which will bring unconscious sin to consciousness. "The message of the True Witness finds the people of God in a sad deception, yet honest in that deception." (3T 253).

If we will remember that the underlying sin of all humanity is participation in the crucifixion of the Son of God (cf. Rom. 3:19; DA 745; TM 38) we are prepared to see that the realization of this sin is buried beneath the surface for the simple reason that fallen men do not accept this conviction (*ouk edokimasan,* Rom. 1:28). And among the professed people of God in these last days there is much confusion about the nature and depth of their sin. "Thou knowest not."

Born of a virgin, Christ did not have the barrier of unconsciousness as we do. Knowing no guilt, He had nothing to repress or "sweep under the rug" as we do. What all men know unconsciously in repression, Christ knew consciously. John spoke of this miracle of the Saviour's inheritance of our true nature and His knowledge of it: "Jesus did not commit Himself unto them, because He knew all men, and needed not that any man should testify of man: for He knew what was in man." (John 2:24, 25).

We are prevented from a full knowledge of our sin because the guilt would kill us. But God "bath made him [Christ] to be sin for us who knew no sin." (2 Cor. 5:21). "The Lord hath laid on Him the iniquity of us all." (Isa. 53:6). (This is surely the opposite of an "exemption"!) Thus John told the truth when he said, "Behold the Lamb of God that taketh away the sin of the world." (John 1:29). It is written that in a unique sense Christ "hated iniquity." (Heb. 1:18). But he could not hate iniquity if He did not understand it. Paul's inspired insight presupposes for Christ a full knowledge of man's unknown mind. Only thus could He understand and bear our iniquity. The "eyesalve" is original with Christ.

If the "angel of the church of the Laodiceans" will receive the "eyesalve" from Christ and use it, he will discern the full truth about himself and about the Saviour. Not only will he gain a full knowledge of his sin, but also a full or complete or "final" atonement for all the sin which is now unknown. The Laodicean message assumes success: "I stand at the door and knock ... I will come in to him, and will sup with him and he with Me." (Verse 20). This is closer intimacy with Christ than has been known by any of the previous six churches. Will the ministry of the High Priest in the Most Holy Apartment ensure this ultimate success? Will Gods people at last truly become like Christ in character? The answer is an unqualified "yes":

> Now, while our great High Priest is making the atonement for us, we should seek to become perfect in Christ. Not even by a thought could our Saviour be brought to yield to the power of temptation. Satan finds in human hearts some point where he can gain a foothold; some sinful desire is cherished by means of which his temptations assert their power. But Christ declared of Himself: " ... the Prince of this world cometh, and hath nothing in Me." (John 14:30) Satan could find nothing in the Son of God that would enable him to gain the victory. He had kept His Fathers commandments, and there was no sin in Him that Satan could use to his advantage. *This is the condition in which those must be found who shall stand in the time of trouble.* (GC 623. emphasis added).

For the first time in history, Laodicea as a corporate body perceives the full dimensions of Calvary in relation to the full dimensions of their own sin. Such a vision would truly annihilate them if they did not "behold Him whom they have pierced." (Zech. 12:10). But they confess and transfer to Christ the now fully conscious conviction of sin and guilt. The "final atonement" solves the conflict in the depths of the heart and guilt is reversed and annihilated. While the saints will still possess a sinful nature and are humble and contrite, sinning comes to an end.

At last the Lamb finds a "wife" who can appreciate Him. His experience of Calvary was the full drinking of the bitter cup of our human guilt. Now His Bride has come to understand and appreciate what He did. Nothing more is required. This at last is "faith" and the result is "righteousness" in harmony with the cleansing of the sanctuary. Is this not the end purpose of the Laodicean message?

An Epilogue:

The Song of Solomon
and the Laodicean Message

There is a hidden love story in the Laodicean message that few of this generation seem ever to have discerned. But thoughtful and reverent students of Scripture have seen it for centuries. Somehow it eluded our pioneers, and our eyes have been too "holden" ever since to see it.

The Greek of Revelation 3:20 reads something like this:

> Behold, I have taken My stand at the door and am knocking. knocking. If a certain one hears My voice and opens the door, I will come in to him and will have intimate relationship with him.

This is a clear allusion to a story in the "Song of Songs" by Solomon, a book that has aroused more embarrassment than thoughtful understanding. The phraseology Christ uses is a direct, exact quotation from the Septuagint, *epi ten thuran*, "at the door," as found in Song of Songs 5:2: "I sleep, but my heart is awake: the voice of my Beloved *knocks at the door* ... " The expression "at the door" is not found in the Hebrew Old Testament for this passage. The editors of the *Seventh-day Adventist Bible Commentary* apparently failed to check the Septuagint which the early church freely used, for they say: "The Song of Solomon is nowhere quoted in the New Testament." (Vol. 3, p. 1111). But it is, here in our Laodicean message by our Lord Himself! Our Lord also referred to it in John 7:38, saying, "He that believeth on Me, as the scripture hath said, ..." referring to Song of Songs

4:12-16, the only Old Testament scripture that He could have referred to. Thus Christ places His stamp of approval on the book and states that its Hero is Himself.

The heroine must therefore be Laodicea herself. And so she is. Her history is clearly delineated therein. It was in the history of 1888 that our Lord "knocked" as a Divine Lover seeking entrance at the door of His Bride-to-be. Jesus' direct quotation from the Septuagint is an inspired commentary that says. "The Laodicean message must be understood in the light of the Song of Solomon." If Christ is not omniscient (He says He does not know the time of His second coming — Mark 13:32), perhaps He did not foreknow the outcome of the 1888 appeal. Can we not appreciate His divine eagerness to take to Himself His Bride-to-be? Can we not sense how Christ "the Lover" hoped against hope that she would respond?

But Ellen White said afterwards, "The disappointment of Christ is beyond description." (*Review and Herald*, Dec. 15, 1904). The Song of Solomon tells what happened better than our own historians have told it. The Bride-to-be is speaking:

A Fruitless Search

I was sleeping, but my heart kept vigil;
   I heard my Lover knocking [at the door. LXX]:
"Open to Me, my sister, My beloved,
   My dove, my perfect one!
For my head is wet with dew,
   My lock with the moisture of the night"

"I have taken off my robe,
   am I then to put it on?
I have bathed my feet,
   am I then to soil them?

"My lover put His hand through the opening;
   my heart trembled within me,
   and I grew faint when He spoke.
I rose to open to my Lover—
   but my Lover had departed, gone.
I sought Him but I did not find Him;
   I called to Him but He did not answer me."
                    (Songs of Songs 5:2-6, New American Bible)

The rest of the chapter pretty well describes our decades of history that have rolled by relentlessly ever since. All this is known to the heavenly universe; only we have stumbled on in blindness and pathetic shame, seeking Him whom we once spurned so tragically:

"The watchmen came upon me
   as they made their rounds of the city;
They struck me, and wounded me,
   and took my mantle from me,
   the guardians of the walls.
I adjure you, daughters of Jerusalem,
   if you find my Lover—
What shall you tell him?—
   that I am faint with love" (verses 7, 8)

What does it mean? "Faint with love" is "sick of love" in the familiar King James Version. The Hebrew word means to be "sick, weak, diseased." It does not mean what we commonly mean as "love-sick," that is, deeply in love. All other uses of that word in the Old Testament mean "diseased".

What does the next verse mean?

The Charms of the Lost Lover

"How does your Lover differ from any other,
   O most beautiful among women?
How does your Lover differ from any other,
   that you adjure us so?" (verse 9).

Is there something distinctive about the Christ whom we will yet learn to love very deeply?

Another word in the Septuagint Song of Songs is arresting. The other women have asked our heroine to tell us why her Lover is so "different" from others. She rhapsodizes on His excellencies in verses 10-16, and then concludes by saying: "Such is my Lover, and such my *friend*, O daughters of Jerusalem." The word translated "friend" is *plesion*, which means "the other one near or close to" in Greek (cf. John 45). What is distinctive about the Christ whom we are to love and proclaim to the world? Ellen White says of the 1888 message:

> On Sabbath afternoon many hearts were touched, and many souls were fed on the bread that cometh down from heaven.. We [she and Jones and Waggoner] felt the necessity of presenting Christ as a Saviour who was not afar off, but *nigh at hand*. (*Review and Herald*, March 5. 1889, emphasis added).

Clearly this is an allusion to the Christology that Jones and Waggoner presented that made Him "nigh," that brought Him truly near as our "kinsman" who came "in the likeness of sinful flesh," "tempted in all points like as we are, yet without sin." There is also a tie-in with Zechariah 12:10 in the Septuagint. The reader will remember the tender passage that describes the close sympathy that God's people will learn to feel for Christ when they realize that He is the One "whom they have pierced." The King James Version says "they shall mourn for Him, as one mourneth for his only son," but the Septuagint reads, "they shall mourn for Him, as for a beloved one," the same word as in the Song of Songs.

Note how Ellen White clearly ties in the Song of Songs phraseology with the results of the 1888 message:

The Christian life, which had before seemed to them [the youth] undesirable and full of inconsistencies, now appeared in its true light, in remarkable symmetry and beauty. He who had been to them as a root out of dry ground, without form or comeliness, became the chiefest among ten thousand. [Song of Songs 5:10] and the one altogether lovely. (*Ibid.*, Feb. 12, 1889)

It is a love story indeed — the most poignant ever penned. It breathes the same hope of ultimate reconciliation and reunion as does the Laodicean message.

Such a hope is worth dying for, and worth living for. Whether our own poor little souls are at last saved and we get to Heaven to bask in our rewards — this is not at all important. What is important is that the deeply disappointed Lover and Bridegroom-to-be receive *His* reward, that *He* at last receive as His Bride a church which is capable of a true heart-appreciation of Him.

Appendix

A Partial Compilation of Ellen White Statements
on Unconscious Sin

Sin is In Us Before Revealed to Consciousness. The Lord places us in different positions to develop us. If we have defects of character of which we are not aware, He gives us discipline that will bring those defects to our knowledge, that we may overcome them. It is His providence that brings us into varying circumstances. In each new position, we meet a different class of temptations. How many times, when we are placed in some trying situation, we think "This is a wonderful mistake. How I wish I had stayed where I was before." But why is it that you are not satisfied? It is because your circumstances have served to bring new defects in your character to your notice; but nothing is revealed but that which was in you. (R&H, Aug. 6, 1889).

Self-deception Lurks in Chamber of the Mind. God's law is the test of our actions. His eye sees every act, searches every chamber of the mind, detecting all lurking self-deception and all hypocrisy. All things are naked and open to the sight of Him with whom we have to do. (Letter 46, 1906; *That I May Know Him*, p. 290).

Peter's Problem with Unconscious Sin Also Ours. The work of restoration can never be thorough unless the roots of evil are reached. Again and again the shoots have been clipped, while the root of bitterness has been left to spring up and defile many; but the very depth of the hidden evil must be reached, the moral senses must be judged, and judged again, in the light of the divine presence. The daily life will testify whether or not the work is genuine. When the third time, Christ said to Peter, "Lovest thou Me?" the probe reached the soul center. Self-judged, Peter fell upon the Rock. (YI, Dec. 22, 1898: 5BC 1152).

The Laodicean Message and Unconscious Sin. The Laodicean message must be proclaimed with power; for now it is especially applicable. ... Not to see our own deformity is not to see the beauty of Christ's character. When we are fully awake to our own sinfulness, we shall appreciate Christ. ... Not to see the marked contrast between Christ and ourselves is not to know ourselves. He who does not abhor himself cannot understand the meaning of redemption. ... There are many who do not see themselves in the light of the law of God. They do not loathe selfishness; therefore they are selfish. (R&H, Sept. 25, 1900).

Unconscious Tendencies to Wrong are Laodicea's Problem. The message to the Laodicean church reveals our condition as a people. ... Satan is seeking with all his subtlety to corrupt mind and heart And O how successful he is in leading men and women to depart from the simplicity of the gospel of Christ! Under his influence hereditary and cultivated tendencies to wrong are roused into activity. Ministers and church-members are in danger of allowing self to take the throne. ... If they would see their defective, distorted characters as they are accurately reflected in the mirror of God's Word, they would be so alarmed that they would fall upon their faces before God in contrition of soul, and tear away the rags of their self-righteousness. (R&H Dec. 15, 1904).

When Unconscious Sin Becomes Conscious Too Late. Those on the left hand of Christ, those who had neglected Him in the person of the poor and the suffering, were unconscious of their guilt. Satan had blinded them; they had not perceived what they owed to their brethren. They had been self-absorbed, and cared not for others' needs. (DA 639).

Moral Machinery of the Heart is Hidden. To men who God designs shall fill responsible positions, He in mercy reveals their hidden defects, that they may look within and examine critically the complicated emotions and exercises of their own hearts, and detect that which is wrong. ... God would have His servants become acquainted with the moral machinery of their own hearts. (4T 85).

Unconscious Sin Fully Conscious at the End. Zechariah's vision of Joshua and the Angel applies with peculiar force to the experience of Gods people in the closing up of the great day of atonement. ... As Joshua was pleading with the Angel, so the remnant church, with brokenness of heart and earnest faith, will plead for pardon and deliverance through Jesus their Advocate. They are fully conscious of the sinfulness of their lives, they see their weakness and unworthiness ... (5T 472, 473).

Sanctuary Services a Type of Removing Unconscious Sin From Mind of Man. The blood of Christ, while it was to release the repentant sinner from the condemnation of the law, was not to cancel the sin; it would stand on record in the sanctuary until the final atonement; so in the type the blood of the sin offering removed the sin from the penitent, but it rested in the sanctuary until the Day of Atonement. In the great day of final award, ... the sins of all the truly penitent will be blotted from the books of heaven. Thus the sanctuary will be freed, or cleansed, from the record of sin. In the type, this great work of atonement or blotting out of sins, was represented by the services of the Day of Atonement. ... As in the final atonement the sins of the truly penitent are to be blotted from the records of heaven, no more to be remembered or come into mind, so in the type they were borne away into the wilderness, forever separated from the congregation. (PP 357, 358).

Satan endeavored to force upon [Jacob] a sense of his guilt, in order to discourage him, and break his hold upon God. ... The heavenly Messenger, in order to try his faith, also reminded him of his sin, and endeavored to escape from him. ... So in the time of trouble, if the people of God had unconfessed sins to appear before them while tortured with fear and anguish, they would be overwhelmed: despair would cut off their faith, and they could not have confidence to plead with God for deliverance. But while they have a deep sense of their unworthiness, they will have no concealed wrongs to reveal. Their sins will have been blotted out by the atoning blood of Christ, and they cannot bring them to remembrance. (PP 201, 202).

Unknown Chapters in Regard to Ourselves. The bitterness of grief and humiliation is better than the indulgences of sin. Through affliction God reveals to us the plague spots in our characters, that by His grace we may overcome our faults. Unknown chapters in regard to ourselves are opened to us, and the test comes, whether we will accept the reproof and the counsel of God. (DA 301).

The Crucifixion of Christ is Man's Unconscious Sin. In the day of final judgment, every lost soul will understand the nature of his own rejection of truth. The cross will be presented, and its real bearing will be seen by every mind that has been blinded by transgression. Before the vision of Calvary with its mysterious Victim, sinners will stand condemned. Every lying excuse will be swept away. Human apostasy will appear in its heinous character. Men will see what their choice has been. ... When the thoughts of all hearts shall be revealed, both the loyal and the rebellious will unite in declaring, "Just and true are Thy ways, Thou King of saints." (DA 58).

How the Unconscious Mind Operated in the Crucifixion of Christ. Believers and unbelievers will fall into line as witnesses to confirm truth that they themselves do not comprehend. All will cooperate in accomplishing the purposes of God, just as did Annas, Caiaphas, Pilate, and Herod. In putting Christ to death, the priests thought they were carrying out their own purposes, but unconsciously and unintentionally they were fulfilling the purpose of God. (R&H, June 12, 1900).

The Judgment Discloses the Hidden Content of the Unconscious Mind. The record of past days will make its disclosure of the vanity of human inventions, by which men have excused themselves for neglecting the claims of God. The Holy Spirit will reveal faults and defects of character that ought to have been discerned and corrected. ... The time is near when the inner life will be fully revealed. All will behold, as if reflected in a mirror, the working of the hidden springs of motive. The Lord would have you now examine your own life, and see how stands your record with Him. (R&H, Nov. 10, 1896).

Sin is Hidden in the Heart. The heart is the treasure-house of sin; not being expelled, it is hidden until an hour of opportunity, and then it is revealed, and springs into action. (Letter H-16f, 1892).

www.ingramcontent.com/pod-product-compliance
Lightning Source LLC
Chambersburg PA
CBHW021119130626
46554CB00002B/767